YOUR SOUL
HAS A PLAN

YOUR SOUL HAS A PLAN

Awaken to Your Life Purpose
through Your Akashic Records

LISA BARNETT

Books may be purchased through booksellers or by contacting Sacred Stories Publishing.

Your Soul Has a Plan
Awaken to Your Life Purpose through Your Akashic Records

Lisa Barnett

Tradepaper ISBN: 978-1-958921-11-1
Electronic Book ISBN: 978-1-958921-12-8

Library of Congress Control Number: 2022947284

Published by Haniel Press
An Imprint of Sacred Stories Publishing, Fort Lauderdale, FL

Printed in the United States of America

Praise for
Your Soul Has a Plan

For thousands of years the indigenous peoples have given prophecies regarding a major shift on the planet. The shift is here now, and collectively human consciousness is becoming higher. Lisa's latest book is the perfect guide for you to understand the Divine purpose of your life and how to access the innate wisdom you already carry within you. Your soul has a plan and is ready to connect with you. Interested? Then this book is for you.

—Lee Carroll,
original Kryon Channel since 1989, author of
17 books translated into more than 25 languages worldwide

—Monika Muranyi,
researcher and Kryon archivist,
author of four Kryon companion books

Your Soul Has a Plan offers you a powerful blueprint to understand your life purpose, along with the support to make changes that will place you fully on the path of your purpose. Through engaging stories and clear action steps, Lisa Barnett shows you how to retrieve your soul's message and follow its guidance for a life of fulfillment.

—Marci Shimoff,
#1 *NY Times* bestselling author, *Happy for No Reason*
and *Chicken Soup for the Woman's Soul*

I'd need to write a whole book to explain how Lisa's work is critical for you and why I'd encourage you to dive in as quickly as possible. Reading Lisa's masterpiece, and deeply considering the wisdom within its pages, is essential. The truth is, taking Lisa's words to heart and applying them is more important than just reading them. Be patient and pause and ponder as you allow the messages to infuse you with love. The world needs *you* to be living your Soul's plan and we, on planet earth, will be uplifted as you are aligned and take actions that fulfill your highest purpose. The guidance in this book will support you. Read and absorb, and in your appreciation for the profound insights you'll have, please also share this book. Buy it as a gift and give it to those you believe in.

—**Kim Serafini**,
CEO & Founder, Positive Prime Technology
& Serafini Mind Spa

I have had the honor and privilege to speak with a lot of people in my life. One of the things that really makes me sad is how few people really know their purpose. And how even fewer realize that over time our purpose can change. Being stuck in what no longer is your purpose is almost as sad as never having found it. Through engaging stories and clear steps, Lisa Barnett's book *Your Soul Has a Plan* shows you how to retrieve your soul's message and follow its guidance for a life of clarity and fulfillment. If you are looking to find your purpose, get this book!

—**Daniel Bruce Levin,**
author of *The Mosaic,* storyteller, and business mystic

Lisa Barnett's *Your Soul Has a Plan* is full of profound wisdom, delivered in accessible, easy-to-digest and implement nuggets of guidance and awareness, gently supporting the reader in coming into conscious alignment with their soul's purpose and divine expression.

—**Ken W. Stone**,
"The Soul Archaeologist," *Experience the Divine Within*

If, like most of us, you wish life came with an instruction manual, you're in luck: bestselling author Lisa Barnett's latest book, *Your Soul Has a Plan*, explains that each of us do, in fact, come into life with a manual. This "Soul Plan" helps us use the skills and experience we've accrued over many lifetimes to grow in awareness and wisdom. Lisa makes it easy to understand why we're here, and how to move forward with purpose.

—Kerri Hummingbird,
#1 international bestselling author of
The Second Wave: Transcending the Human Drama

This is not your mother's "how-to" book. This knowledge comes directly from the Akashic Masters via Lisa's highly developed ability to receive their messages on our behalf. The guidance is practical and will allow you to understand why it's not necessary to repeat the same challenges and traumatic lessons over and over again.

—Debra Poneman,
Founder and President, Yes to Success, Inc.

Reading Lisa's book is a deep dive into the most precious part of your being. *Your Soul Has a Plan* is a guide for your journey into self, and Lisa shares the extensive gifts of the Akashic Records very personally with you! She takes you on a soul journey that shows you how to work with past lives and talents, heal trauma, and bring your innate gifts into your life now, as a blessing for yourself and others.

Lisa and I have a deep and ancient soul connection over many thousands of years/lives, playing in the Akasha. This book is a blessing for your life and our times.

—Lumari,
internationally acclaimed spiritual coach,
creation catalyst, multi-dimensional channel, Akashic expert,
international bestselling author

Lisa's latest book, *Your Soul Has a Plan*, is the perfect remedy for these confusing and often challenging times, providing a clear instruction manual for your life. You will be guided every step of the way to turn obstacles into opportunities, dreams into reality.

—Wendy Darling,
personal and business transformational results expert,
Miraculous Living Institute

DEDICATION

I dedicate this book to all the awakening souls
on the planet today and
those who are on their way.
Many have sought guidance
through the Akashic Records and
I'm grateful to you for your desire to awaken
and heal our world.
You have been my spiritual inspiration,
opening doors with your questions and
expanding our view of life
as we received guiding wisdom and
unconditional love along with
these healing prayers from the Akashic Masters.
Thank you for assisting in the healing of us all.

TABLE OF CONTENTS

FOREWORD

It was November of 2012 and I was completing my first year hosting *Your Life Without Limits*, an audio interview show that was a forerunner to the webinar/summit craze that exploded mid-decade. This then-innovative format utilized FreeConferenceCall.com so that I could bring some of the most renowned thought leaders in the world directly onto your cordless home phone—or computer, if you were savvy enough to figure out how to actually log in to the show without it dropping.

My guests included everyone from Bernie Siegel to Norman Cousins, from Jack Canfield to Access Consciousness' Dain Heer—even stars of *The Secret* such as Marci Shimoff, Michael Beckwith, and Marie Diamond.

I have no recollection of how I came to interview this uniquely exotic and beautiful woman named Lisa Barnett, who was edgy even for a show called *Your Life Without Limits*. She did something called "reading your Akashic Records." Meeting her was a turning point in my life.

The way I understood it, our Akashic Records are kept by beings of light who are here for all of us, to assist our journey through this lifetime and help us gain clarity into our soul's unique plan.

When I met Lisa, she already had more than twenty years of experience accessing the ancient healing wisdom of the Akashic field by using sacred prayers given to her by the Lords of the Akashic Records. She was even able to successfully teach others to access their own personal Akashic Records and uncover their own soul's plan!

My first interview with Lisa was eye-opening. I was hooked. I mean, who wouldn't want beings of light to guide you on your soul's journey?

Lisa's show was one of the most popular, out of more than 200 shows I hosted. Now, ten years later, Lisa and the beings of light are still generously guiding me. They always seem to show up at just the right time with exactly the information I need to take my life to the next level.

Case in point. . . .

Right after our first interview in 2012, I had a personal Akashic Record reading with Lisa. I was happily ensconced in my life in Chicago, living within a stone's throw of my two adult children. I had no intention of going anywhere. But the Record Keepers had a different idea.

"You're going to be moving to the Bay Area," they said through Lisa.

"Not a chance," I replied. "I have never had the tiniest desire to live in that area of the country. Maybe southern California, but never northern."

"I'm just sharing what the Record Keepers are telling me."

I inwardly rolled my eyes, thinking I knew better.

Within the next few months, my son had unexpectedly moved to New York; my daughter was accepted to chiropractic college in the Bay Area; and I'd founded a business with a dear friend, also in the Bay Area. The moving van was already on the way!

That was just one of many priceless encounters that has solidified my fan-girl obsession with Lisa and the books and teachings that she offers—and I am certain that her current book, *Your Soul Has a Plan*, is her best work yet.

This book gives you the understanding of how to live in the

flow of life from a higher perspective and to create your own future by engaging your soul's plan. It shows you how to work through old karmic patterns to make room for the abundance that is your birthright. It guides you to release unneeded, old emotional pain, not only from this life but from previous incarnations.

This is not your mother's "how-to" book. This guidance is coming from the Akashic Masters via Lisa's well-developed ability to receive their messages on our behalf. The knowledge is practical and will show you why you don't have to repeat the same challenges and traumatic lessons over and over.

I have no doubt that *Your Soul Has a Plan* will open your eyes to a new realm of experience. Reading Lisa's words will allow you to begin to live a life of greater happiness, more radiant health, deeper love, and a profound understanding of why you incarnated now—at this interesting and challenging time in the history of humankind.

—**Debra Poneman**
Founder and President, Yes to Success, Inc.

INTRODUCTION

Humans have asked, begged, cajoled, and bargained with the Divine to answer the most basic and important questions about life on Earth: Who am I? Why am I here? Is this all there is?

These questions are like carrots we chase to find answers about our identity and purpose on Earth.

You Are an Ancient Traveler

You are so much more than a human being. You are a quantum soul having a human experience on many levels: emotionally, mentally, physically, and spiritually. As an ancient traveler, you move throughout space and time, and you have lived on Earth hundreds of times. You've been involved in thousands of relationships. You are here now to live fully, with purpose and love.

I want you to know that you are much more than your physical body. You are a magnificent, expansive soul; your soul chose this pivotal time in human history because your love and wisdom are needed to help humanity birth a new age, the Age of Aquarius.

Many astrologers see the Age of Aquarius as the time when humanity takes back control of the Earth and the destiny of humanity. This period of time is represented by the constellation of stars known as Aquarius, the eleventh constellation of the zodiac.

If you're old enough to remember the musical *Hair*, performed on stage in 1967, you are likely part of the first wave of Lightworkers. These souls were born between 1940 and 1970. They came to assist in ending war and creating a time of peace on Earth.

Even if you are part of one of the later waves that followed, you most likely were inspired, as a soul, to come to Earth so you could be part of this transformational time. It is taking humanity longer than we had hoped to move from war to peace, from hate to love, from fear to trust. It is good to know this new age will last about 2,160 years and bring us into a golden era. This will be the time when there is enough energetic light coming to Earth to help humanity raise our consciousness and create peace.

You are reading this book because you're here to support humanity's transformation and help us all to heal our beautiful planet.

Welcome, fellow traveler.

I Want to Introduce You to Your Very Own Akashic Record Keepers

The beings of light who are in service to you will assist your soul's journey through this lifetime. They will help you gain insights and clarity into your soul's plan. I call them the Akashic Record Keepers or Akashic Masters. They feel unconditional love for you, wanting to support and guide you by providing specific information, ancient wisdom, healing energy, and guidance to make your journey through this lifetime much more expansive.

Their assistance can help you clear personal trauma, emotional pain, and fear so that you can experience daily fulfillment. I've seen thousands of people worldwide move from feeling emotionally broken and financially broke to experiencing love, financial abundance, and the ability to recognize and share their soul's gifts and talents. The possibilities are endless with the insight and understanding of your soul's plan.

A Message from the Akashic Record Keepers

When the Akashic Record Keepers first asked me to help them bring this soul wisdom back to humanity, they explained this during a channeling session:

Dear Ones,

We have always been with you, although much of humanity is unaware of us. We are the Beings of Light of the Akasha. We are pure Source energy and have never been human. We have been in service to all souls throughout time. We are the Keepers of the soul recordings in the great libraries of the Akashic Field. We have no judgment of the human experience and are solely here to guide you. It is your birthright to access the wisdom and gifts you have acquired from your hundreds and thousands of lifetimes on Earth and other dimensional planes.

Over one thousand years ago, we removed access to the Akasha from most humans. It was referred to as "The Dark Ages" because there was a minimal amount of Energetic Light on Earth, allowing Dark energy to rule, making it dangerous to speak or share the wisdom and power of ancient tools. Those who could access the guidance of the Akashic Field misused the information by using it for personal gain. We, the Akashic Record Keepers, withdrew the energy and access away from Earth so humanity could no longer have access to the guidance.

As we enter this New Age, sometimes referred to as The Age of Aquarius, we know it is time to return to humanity's ability to access soul wisdom. Many who read these words have a soul commitment to assist in helping others awaken to higher consciousness and help with the healing of your Mother Earth, Gaia.

This ancient wisdom, stored in Source energy and the Quantum field, is here for you. It will support your soul growth by assisting you to access your Soul Plan in the Akashic Record. We are delighted to speak with you today to share information to help your path to awakening.

How to Use this Book

Welcome and thank you for allowing us to take this journey with you in discovering your soul's plan, or at least to help start you on your path to finding who you are as a soul.

The Akashic Record Keepers and I will share information to help you to better understand your soul, its plan, karma, your soul purpose, and your vital life lessons. We know you have come to help humanity awaken to their light and evolve into the next level of consciousness. You are also preparing to embrace the higher energy of the Age of Aquarius.

Each chapter has three roles in guiding and assisting you. In the first part, we will teach you. In the second part, we offer questions for reflection and inspiration. Finally, we share our healing prayers to facilitate alignment with your soul's plan and purpose.

We teach the concepts of creating a soul plan through examples and stories. Also, self-discovery questions are provided to help you become more aware of and let go of stuck emotions, karmic patterns, and emotional trauma. Finally, the Akashic Healing Prayers are included at the end of each chapter to assist in the release of old, unnecessary emotional pain and unconscious beliefs.

Let's Start with a Few Concepts We'll Talk About in this Book

- First, you are so much more than you perceive yourself to be.

- Your soul created a plan before you incarnated.

- Your soul's expansive wisdom is available and valuable to you.

- Your soul family is here to support and assist you with your plan.

- You can benefit from reading this book even if you don't yet know anything about your soul plan or understand how it can help you in your life. This book will help you understand how your challenges, emotional trauma, or old emotional issues can stand in the way of living a purposeful life. Once you get into the flow of soul energy, the magic happens.

- We have added journaling pages toward the end of the book to reflect on the Exercise for Reflection in each chapter, to note your favorite prayers, and to make observations for your soul's growth. Journaling is a helpful way to be conscious of your thoughts and feelings as you transform.

- We intend to help you understand your life from a higher perspective, from the soul's expansiveness. Taking in the vastness of the soul's experiences will improve your understanding and help you to make new choices that engage your soul's plan. We also wish to help you release unwanted emotional pain so you can be free from childhood and past-life trauma.

- We are ready to take this journey with you. As your Akashic Record Keepers, we will meet you where you are.

Enjoy your journey!

CHAPTER 1

YOU WERE BORN
WITH A MANUAL

B efore you begin, I'd like to share a message from the Akashic
Beings of Light:

*Welcome. We invite you to step into the Akashic energy field
with us. As we guide you through this book, you will notice
your life alter and evolve. As you work with the exercises and
prayers, you will feel old constrictions released, making life
easier. As you work with this practice, you will see doorways
open where once there were blank walls.*

*We will work with you through the high vibration of
Akashic Energy, which comes to you as you read. We will
support and assist you in clearing old, stuck energy in your
life to move out of fear and into a space of love and faith. We
are your Akashic Record Keepers and pure Beings of Light.
Our sole purpose is to guide you on this journey. Remember,
you are never alone. You are connected to us and Creator/
Source at all times. Please feel this in your heart when we*

say, We are here to support you. Remember that we are pure Source energy. We have never been human and hold no judgment toward the human condition or situations. As you connect with us, you connect to the infinite power of love. You are safe and loved.

My question is, "Have you ever wondered why you are here and what your purpose is?"

The exciting answer is . . . . You created a plan before coming to Earth that holds much of the information you are searching for. But unfortunately, many of us don't remember our plan, and we spend much of our life trying to figure out why we're here.

My Soul Had a Plan

I can remember not being in a body, roaming the galaxies as an etheric soul, easily conversing with two other souls in another dimension. My etheric form was free and agile, moving with the slightest thought. But that all came to a thundering halt when I was three years old, as I realized I was stuck here on Earth, trapped in a body again!

I can remember looking at my hands and being startled. The reality shook me as it filled my little body with fear. Not having the vocabulary to tell my mom why her little girl was so panicked, all I could say was, "I want to go home." I was filled with tears and confusion. My mother told me everything was fine, and that I *was* home. It didn't matter; I kept repeating that I wanted to return home.

I consider myself lucky because that memory, from age three, informed my whole life. It has guided me to seek answers so I can understand at a deeper, more meaningful level: Why was I in a body again? What was my plan? And why did I come here?

When I was a teenager, I had an insatiable hunger to learn about esoteric and spiritual studies. I read every book I could find on the subject. In college, I studied philosophy. But the more I knew, the more questions I had.

Then my search took a sharp turn, creating a desperate need to find meaning in my life.

At thirteen, one of my two soul sisters—who was my best friend—went into a coma. I felt her healing was my responsibility; somehow, it was my calling to heal her. I didn't know how to pray because my household wasn't religious; even so, I prayed all night to save her life by pulling her from the coma.

I felt responsible when my prayers didn't work. She died the next day.

My other soul sister, Shuby, died suddenly in a car accident during college. It haunted me, as I also felt responsible for that death, because I hadn't been there to save her—even though I lived in California and she lived in Illinois. Why would I think I had a responsibility to heal my friends? It didn't make any sense to me.

Therapists might say that this was a normal reaction to losing someone close. However, I've learned that there is another answer: We are all ancient and entangled souls. My feeling of being responsible for them ignited part of my soul's path as a healer.

By my teen years, I knew I had been a healer in hundreds of lifetimes. Because that was and is who I am at a soul level, my internal knowing believed I could heal my friends, and I could have saved Shuby if I had been in Illinois rather than California.

Has something similar ever happened to you? You might sense that you can do something you've never done or believe you have a special gift or ability, even though you haven't been trained or taught how to do it.

The Akashic Record Keepers say this happens because we have used that gift or talent many times before, in past lives. We have come to Earth as ancient souls with a plan, whether easy or challenging, and with the desire to unlock our long-forgotten talents, gifts, and experiences so we can heal ourselves and others.

We come equipped with the tools to do the work we are here to do.

Our biggest challenge is allowing our talents to show themselves.

Your Soul's Plan

So often, when we feel isolated, alone, or lonely, we think we don't have a purpose. Yet we feel there must be something more to life than what we're experiencing! I want you to know that you do have a purpose. You produced a plan detailing all kinds of experiences, karmic lessons, life purposes, trials and tribulations, relationships, career choices, and so on.

You made plans for different types of relationships with more than twenty-five people worldwide. For example, you wrote contracts with people who would become significant love partners, business partners, friends, parents, children, or siblings.

Some of these relationships come from your original soul family, and others don't. For example, our parents aren't always part of our soul family; in some lifetimes, we don't even have a social contract with them. I'll explain more about your original soul family in Chapter 3.

Your soul has so much knowledge and information you can use to navigate this lifetime. The reasoning behind your soul choices becomes more apparent as you learn more about your soul's plan and dive deeper into finding answers to why you are here.

I Wish My Child Came with a Manual

When I was raising my three children, I belonged to two parent groups, including serving as the president of the Mothers of Multiples Club. When my twins were born, I felt insecure about parenting them. I'll never forget how often I heard a new mother say, "I wish my child came with a manual!"

As new parents, we all feel lost and unsure about why our

babies are crying so much, or colicky, not sleeping through the night, or even why they were born with a physical challenge. We often blame ourselves because we don't have answers.

I've seen how reassuring it is to realize that life is not random. We make choices to learn and grow. We experience struggles, love, and hopefully joy during each lifetime.

Dream Your Soul's Desire

Do you dream big, only to settle for small? Some people have big dreams and goals to meet, but they stop because they believe they are not worthy of such grandeur. You might think that your dreams are outlandish or crazy! But, when you realize who you are as an ancient soul, your dreams will become grounded in the truth of who you have been in other lifetimes. You will see that these dreams are an extension from where you left off.

There was nothing more exciting for me than realizing my dream of publishing. The book you have in your hands is my third. Each time I publish another book, I'm in awe that my dream of sharing ancient wisdom through writing has become a reality. From a soul's perspective, writing and publishing books were in my soul's plan to expand my purpose and to share this work with the world.

The same goes for you. If you dream of writing, it might be because you have authored many books in other lifetimes. We can even connect with information from our past lives as published authors, to assist us in creating and publishing a new book. For example, one of my clients who was drafting a book discovered, in her Akashic Records, that the characters in her book were her from unfinished lifetimes when she had died suddenly.

Writing is part of my soul plan and a dream of mine. So, what are some of your grandest, seemingly impossible dreams? Your soul plan is waiting for you to discover its information about the gifts you can reclaim from past lives in which you were a skillful expert with the talents to make your dreams reality.

EXERCISE FOR REFLECTION

One of the quickest, most direct paths to align with your soul is through your big, beautiful, and magnificent heart. If you dedicate yourself to learning how to open your heart to receive wisdom, messages, and healings, you will change your life and how you experience the world. This might be the key to all you seek.

Column of Light Meditation

The Akashic Masters offer a simple visual meditation to assist in connecting to them through your heart. They wish you to feel your connection from within your heart. This meditation was created to do so:

1. *Please close your eyes with your feet flat on the floor. Focus your attention on your connection to your dear mother Earth solidly beneath your feet. Bring your focus from your feet slowly up to your heart, always breathing deeply into your heart.*

2. *See your heart open, ever-expanding. Relax into the expansion, allowing your heart to fill with the feelings of unconditional love. Stay there until you feel it fully. Breathe into the continued expansion of your heart.*

3. *Now move your attention and the energy up into your head, the area between your eyebrows, moving back into the center of your head, until you see a small master gland, your pineal gland. Spend time with it.*

4. *Thank it for all the work it does to assist your body. Send love from your heart to your pineal, for it is the energy center that connects to your higher self, your soul, and eventually to us, the Guardians of the Akashic Records and the Masters from Source. Your connection is how we can communicate with you.*

5. *See and feel the energy flow from Earth up through your feet. Let it rise up into your heart and move up to connect your heart to your pineal gland. Pay attention to energy rising from your pineal gland to the top of your head, making the connection up to us.*

6. *Imagine a silvery blue column of light coming from us to connect to you. The column surrounds your whole body and continues down into the Earth. You are surrounded and protected by the Akashic Column of Light the Record Keepers and Beings of Light sent you. Inside the column of light, you are held in Divine love.*

7. *Take a few moments to feel your connection to unconditional love or behold the spectacular sight of you being surrounded and protected in the silvery blue column. Breathe in unconditional love. Know you are guided and always have been.*

8. *Inside this connection, you can transform your life with the healing prayers of the Akashic Records. Relax into the healing energy as you recite the prayers. Feel their source energy running through you, surrounding you, filling you with lasting love.*

9. *When you feel complete, you may go about your day, confident the healing is taking place.*

PRAYER FOR CREATING YOUR DREAMS

I am clear. I am focused. I am ready to do whatever it takes to make my dreams come true. I know that my clarity with the assistance of Akashic Records creates miracles in my life.

I am seen, heard, and recognized for the gifts and talents I offer.

The universe conspires with me to make magic happen, and my dreams come true.

So it is. Blessed Be.

PRAYER TO ACCESS CREATIVITY

Mother, Father, Goddess, God, I Am awakened, creative energy.

As I breathe into my heart, I ignite my creative energy.

I see it spinning threads of gold light.

As this golden ball of light spins ever faster within my chest,

I activate the connection to my creative energy rings, which slowly turn above my head.

Please assist me in merging the strength of my creative energy in my heart with the creative energy of the universe.

As these energies merge, I feel them spin as one, flowing through my head down into my heart and back up again. I ask for creative ideas to assist in my life. I am blessed and filled with gratitude.

Let's jump in and learn more about the plan your soul wrote, which will assist you in fulfilling your soul's purpose.

CHAPTER 2

WHY AM I HERE?
= SOUL PLAN

E ach time we decide to reincarnate to Earth, our soul creates a plan we will uncover during that lifetime. We make our plans as infinite souls desiring to do great things in our lifetimes. These plans identify which gifts, talents, challenges, and other souls we will encounter in the upcoming lifetime. In addition, we carry with us some soul contracts and karmic patterns to learn from, including soul family members to support us in uncovering those patterns.

One Life or More?

Many people and religions believe that we live only one life. I've always wondered why some people have an easy life with a comfortable home, plenty of money, and a lovely family while others live in extreme poverty in undeveloped countries, struggling for every bite of food they eat or suppressed by radical cultural dogma.

I can't believe we only have one life! If that were the case, it would be a random drawing to see if we could be rich or poor, healthy or sick, wise or mentally challenged. Life seems so much more complicated than one spin of the lottery wheel.

Let's Unpack This a Little More

Would we blame ourselves or God for our bad luck if we only lived one life? Would it matter if we learned and grew if we never returned to Earth? There wouldn't be any karmic stories to bring us together in another life, and we wouldn't have soul contracts to complete in our relationships. We would be "one and done" with our random experiences. It seems like a waste of a beautiful planet with so much to offer.

What about the karma we create in that one lifetime? People often think of karma as punishment; if true, wouldn't we need to live many lives to accumulate enough karma to create a difficult life? Also, if we have one life, does God randomly choose the type of life we get to live? Again, that would seem like some people would be punished and some rewarded—but for what?

None of these scenarios make sense to me. Life is full of many twists and turns and serendipitous events. People are born with talents far beyond their age's capabilities. Think of musical and math prodigies. It makes more sense to me that we bring past-life skills into other incarnations so we can share them with more people.

You Are Here to Learn

I don't believe that the circumstances of our lives are random or that we only have one life to live. My experiences and the guidance I've received is that most of us have lived hundreds of lifetimes here on our beautiful planet Earth.

When you start to think that you've had hundreds and hundreds of lifetimes, then the idea that you have had many jobs learning numerous skills to create a successful life could make sense. Success comes from multiple attempts to excel, as we challenge ourselves to master our thoughts, emotions, and deeds.

Historical movies remind us of all the challenges humanity has experienced throughout history. So many people struggle to feel loved and to love, to be kind, and to feel abundant, worthy, and generous as humans. Can you imagine how we might choose a challenging life to learn the soul lessons of pain, forgiveness, and love?

Essential Benefits of Soul Work

When you write your soul's plan, you look at the many natural gifts and talents you've developed and those that still need mastering. You consider everything that will assist you in completing your life's purpose.

When I give an Akashic Record consultation, I guide clients through quantum past-life work to reclaim these gifts and talents. As a result, their consultation becomes a powerful tool to support them in feeling capable of starting a new project or going in a new direction. They might want to create a new business, find a relationship, build a career, learn a unique talent, or jump into doing something completely different. They want to do so many things, but they are afraid they aren't skilled enough.

This example is one of the essential benefits of soul work. Understanding your soul's plan can assist you in creating the life that you desire. Many people find it easier to relax when they know that other souls are here to support them on their journey. We make soul contracts with best friends, children, business partners, significant life partners, and with those who will create other supportive relationships.

When you realize that you *planned* what you're experiencing in your life right now, and when you take responsibility for your choices, it helps you to stop blaming others for life's circumstances.

We are responsible for identifying new ways to be the creators of our lives by making new choices when the old ones aren't working for us anymore.

You Wrote a Plan to Guide You

In *The Immutable Laws of the Akashic Field*, Laszlo writes: "The Akashic Field is a cosmic field in which all information and knowledge are interconnected and preserved. Our reality is anchored in this vast sea of information that gives rise to everything . . . from specks of stardust in the outer cosmos to consciousness itself."

You wrote your soul plan in the quantum field of energy so you could grow and discover why you decided to be born at this time. We might talk about karma in connection to personal and soul growth, but your plan has much more information for you to discover.

It's vital to know that your soul plans are malleable. You can change the choices you made eons ago. Along with your soul plan, you have free will, which is an important component of who you are and what you become. You have chosen a path, but you can still decide what you want to create in your life.

As a very ancient and wise soul, you considered your different lifetimes and decided what would be beneficial to learn and which gifts and talents you'd like to share this time.

We are living through an unusual time in history. So many souls have come back to Earth to help humanity create a new and empowering world where everyone can thrive. You might already realize it is possible to consciously transform life on Earth by recognizing the many lives you've lived and the experiences you've gathered over the millennia.

Your soul holds ancient wisdom, information, and memories from other lifetimes and dimensions that are always available to you as you self-actualize.

A Soul Plan Has Valuable Information

Our soul plan can include many contracts, vows, karmic lessons, gifts, talents you want to share, and abilities you are ready to release to bring in more potential. Here is just a sampling of some of the experiences we might include in our soul's plan for any one lifetime:

- Contracts with people to support each other

- Contracts with people to grow (karmic contracts)

- Contracts with parents, siblings, children, and other family members

- Contracts to have children, which may or may not actualize

- Contracts with the children you have, which may be your children by birth or adopted or stepchildren

- Group contracts to serve a higher purpose together

- Group contracts with your family or spiritual group

- Gifts you want to share with humanity

- Talents to rediscover

- Karmic patterns to learn from and release

- Karmic growth

Why Do We Come Back to Earth?

Each time we come to Earth, we make a new soul plan, including the lessons we want to learn to ensure soul growth. Our contracts, karma, and love for humanity and ourselves give us a glimpse into the big question: "Why am I here?"

We also love this beautiful, blue-and-green planet for its physical aspects. We want to feel the pleasure of eating great food, relaxing in the sunshine, making love, raising babies, smelling flowers, touching everything, and having all the fabulous experiences we can feel with our bodies.

We are large, expansive, and wise souls when making our souls' plans. Time and space do not limit us. Each lifetime might include quite different experiences; we can be rich in one life and poor in another. As infinite souls, these challenges and obstacles don't scare us because we understand that life on Earth is short. It's over in the blink of an eye. We know each challenge we overcome is essential to our soul's growth.

Why Choose Challenges and Obstacles?

As your soul evolves, it can go to other worlds and dimensions, sharing its Earth experiences. Think of it as progressing in school. You start with preschool and can work your way up to a Ph.D. You choose how far you want to go. It's determined by what you plan for this lifetime.

When people channel spirit guides, they often channel souls who have finished their time in Earth School and have transitioned to a mission of helping others. Some of these souls work as groups of galactic beings, wise guides, and ascended masters dedicated to helping us gain answers to our questions of who we are and why we are here as ancient souls.

I'll Go with You

Each time your soul comes to Earth, you make your plan to progress as much as possible, which can be challenging in human form. Picture a gymnasium full of souls looking for partners, children, siblings, business partners, cultural experiences, war, love, and any experience you can create. You are all calling out, "Who wants to be my significant other?" or "Who wants to be my child?" These will be the souls coming back to Earth to fulfill their contracts with you.

Hands go up, and the conversation begins. One soul might come up to you and say, "Remember when we were married, lifetimes ago, and then I died in a runaway carriage accident? You vowed to love me forever. Let's get married again to have a long life together."

You say, "Yes," and then move on to the next person.

They say, "Remember when you were my alcoholic husband? That relationship created some karma for both of us. You didn't learn to be present and love unconditionally, and I had anger issues. Let's try again and finish the karmic lesson now."

You agree and move on to the next person.

"We had a long and beautiful marriage, 700 years ago. Shall we try that again? It was lovely."

You remember and agree before you move on to the next person.

You now have ten soul contracts with people who want to be your spouse or significant other. That seems like a lot, since you might want to marry only once. However, if you don't have a lot of contracts, you might never meet the *one love* you desire, so you hedge your bets by making many contracts.

Finishing Contracts

You might quickly finish the contract with your past life partner when you were an alcoholic. In this life, neither of you drink; you share your feelings and even go to a therapist to work out some childhood issues. You feel loved and seen. This completes the karma, so you no longer need to stay together. The purpose of that connection was learning to communicate with a significant partner instead of hiding behind alcohol. Those soul lessons were meant to help you to evolve into a more loving partner and become better suited for your heart's desire and your soul growth.

As time passes in this new lifetime, you meet and marry the person you had a long and beautiful marriage with hundreds of years ago. This marriage contract doesn't include children; you raise fur babies. You might have come to do collective work balancing Divine Feminine and Divine Masculine energies, which entails being a mother of many, such as nieces and nephews or the neighbors' children, instead of being a biological mother to children.

Now you've connected with two of the ten contracts you made for significant partners in this life, and that piece of your soul plan is complete. You even completed one contract with karma attached; that's what soul growth looks like in your life. And on you go, sharing the gifts you planned to share and spreading love by supporting and completing your remaining soul contracts with others.

Many Interpretations

When expanding your awareness and answering the questions offered on these pages, remember, there is never just one answer or a right or wrong one. Instead, each question has many interpretations regarding your soul's path.

As ancient souls, numerous lifetimes can create layered connections to each karmic issue, contract, and vow based on what we chose to heal this time around. Likewise, karmic patterns connect us with many other soul agreements to develop in life. Our quest is to complete as many as possible and to enjoy a life blessed with fulfilled dreams.

EXERCISE FOR REFLECTION

1. Close your eyes and take a few deep breaths to open your heart.

2. Imagine a library with books filling shelves from floor to ceiling and as far as your eyes can see. These volumes represent different lifetimes.

3. See them attended to and cared for by your personal librarians. Begin to feel the presence of Divine and unconditional love. Feel the energetic vibrational presence of knowledge from the words, actions, and deeds of the lifetimes you've lived.

4. Allow yourself to stand in the vibration of knowing your soul's truth. Know that you are in an extraordinary place of guidance, ancient wisdom, and information ready to assist you in experiencing joy and fulfillment every day.

5. Open your heart with gratitude and let the energetic vibration of love and knowledge fill your being. Feel that every cell of your body comes alive as you acknowledge that you are where you need to be.

6. Say your goodbyes for now as you gently return to the work you are about to do.

What did you experience?

PRAYER OF REMEMBRANCE

As I know the truth of my Divinity,

I begin to have an experience of myself as one who knows.

I know myself as the ancient and wise soul that I am.

I am aligned with my True Self and the manifestation of all things.

My body and soul are healed and enlivened by the Light of the Divine.

I am expansive. I am love.

So it is. Blessed Be.

PRAYER OF KNOWING

Mother, Father, Goddess, God, I am now electing to know the Truth of my Divinity.

As I do, I have an experience of myself as one who knows my connection to higher consciousness.

I align with my ability to hear guidance from my soul.

I receive this authority with grace.

I now know myself as a Divine Child of the Creator and claim my Divine gifts.

So it is. Blessed Be.

PRAYER OF SELF LOVE

Mother, Father, Goddess, God, as I now choose to move from my head, deeply into my heart, I connect to my love of self.

This sacred room holds the memory of the Divine in me.

There is nothing else.

I sit calmly in my heart center and feel the pervasive energy of the Creator.

I am that I Am.

Blessed Be.

In the next chapter, you'll learn how your soul contracts affect your relationships.

CHAPTER 3

RELATIONSHIPS = SOUL CONTRACTS

When we write our soul plan, a big part of the plan is to be in a relationship with other souls. We want to support them, share our love and lives, and learn from them.

Since we want to be productive in our lives, not just living a random existence, we write our plan to include soul contracts with others interested in accomplishing similar tasks or those who volunteer to help us learn or complete a karmic pattern.

Many people come to me worried they won't have another contract for a significant partner if they leave their relationship. Some people believe we have one soul mate or "twin flame" and are worried that they haven't found "the one" yet.

The Record Keepers say that most of us write six to twelve contracts with people to have significant partnerships. There are a few reasons we write so many. First, if we only have one soul mate or if we wrote only one soul contract for a life partner, most of us would be single. We might never find that one person on this giant planet. They could be living on the other side of the world or in the same city, but we might still never cross paths.

Sometimes we meet a person with whom we have a contract, but they are already happily married. That is why we must have other soul contracts.

I've done thousands of readings for people who come to me with relationship questions. For example, they might feel they have grown apart after twenty or thirty years of marriage. The client wants to know if their contract is completed and if they will create any karma if they get divorced. The Record Keepers sometimes say that the contract is incomplete. They might offer suggestions on how to complete it or work toward healing it. They often say the purpose of the contract has been met for many years, and the client needs to continue consciously on their soul path.

Many of my clients are lightworkers, healers, and soul guides who are on Earth to help us awaken. It's important to release the old energies that hold us back; sometimes, divorce or separation might be the best choice.

The Record Keepers will often say, *The person still has one, two, or three soul contracts for a significant love partner left.* Even my clients in their sixties and seventies have available contracts.

Remember, you may have written twelve contracts to have a life partner, and you've only used one or two. Possibly a few of the souls you contracted with are in marriages or have crossed over, but you might still have a few contracts available.

We are great at planning, as we have had hundreds of lifetimes to practice. We wish to ensure we have enough options for love and life partners. We also include soul contracts for parents, siblings, grandparents, aunts, and uncles in our planning. We usually pick our family members because of their souls, but sometimes it's for the genealogy we will get from the parents.

Before we're born, we see life and families differently. It isn't always about completing karmic relationships or patterns. Most of us have soul contracts with Mom and Dad, although many are with just one parent, sibling, or family member.

It is rare, but occasionally we've been part of a family lineage in a past life. We might wish to connect to its genes and the gifts and talents held in that family line. We can choose to come back into that family for their abilities and genes.

Our soul contracts don't stop with our family or life partners. We may write a contract with karma attached, so that our soul can learn. Our karma contracts are often with our family or significant partner. But mainly, we write *Support Contracts*. We come to support other souls, and they return the favor by helping us on our journey. They might be our best friend, business partner, or mother-in-law. A support contract is the perfect type of marriage contract. It's good to know that even if you have a support contract with someone, it doesn't mean there will be no soul growth or challenges in those relationships. Remember, soul growth is our primary objective.

What is a Soul Family?

In the previous chapter, I shared an example of a soul plan and how we determine what we'll do in our upcoming life. Let's expand our knowledge on soul plans.

Take a moment to imagine when there was no space or time. You are a part of Source with no history or identity. And then your soul decides to individuate from Source.

The Akashic Record Keepers love to share ideas as parables. Here is the story they told me when I first asked about what happens when an aspect of Source decides to individuate and become a singular soul:

> *Imagine Source as a tall, energetic, high-rise building in New York City. At one point, the energy to become you chooses to individuate from the Source. This energy gathers with a group of Souls who also decide to individuate simultaneously. All want to know what it feels like to become an individual, make choices, and understand what self means without Source.*

As the first step, all of you get into an elevator at the top of the high-rise. You are moving toward individuating, and this small group of new souls becomes your soul family. As you ride the elevator toward the ground floor, you share hopes and dreams of your journeys in becoming a soul family. When you arrive at the lobby level, you are entirely individual. A plan begins, formulating the following steps as a soul family. Each of you is curious about all the experiences and possibilities in a multi-verse filled with so much.

Where shall we explore? What shall we do? How do we move forward? When will we meet again? What's next?

So many questions, so much wonder, and curiosity. Since none of you have experience outside of Source, you decide to stroll down the avenue, taking in all the activity from your senses.

As you walk, you see a large structure, one block square, about five stories high. Curious, all of you go inside to discover what answers it has to offer. After entering, you can't help but notice the numerous balconies surrounding an expansive atrium at the center of the building. You see thousands of books on each terrace, floor after floor. All of you look up as you circle around, taking it all in. It's breathtaking. Piqued with curiosity about what those books may share, it's decided to stay, study, and get the answers all you seek to the many questions you have.

You have all learned what possibilities lie ahead for the next part of your journeys, together and separately. Some go their own way quickly, and some of us stay and help in the library. You continue learning and understanding the world as you are in service to many souls.

The large building with thousands of books represents our Akashic Record library and is an example of what is available to all of us within it. Our soul's library is part of Source vibration and holds all the memories and recordings of everything throughout time. Every thought, word, deed, and energetic resonance of our experiences fills our books.

Each soul decides what their plan will be, and off they go to rediscover what they planned so long ago.

Of course, in this parable, the Record Keepers have presented a simplified version of how life begins for each of us as an individuated Soul of Source.

Do I Only Have Relationships with My Soul Family?

In the example given by the Akashic Record Keepers, when we individuate, our Soul Family begins to form. About twenty-five souls come down the etheric elevator together. We begin as grand and expansive souls, but as we journey through galaxies, dimensions, and lives in the various realms, we write different soul plans. Each soul grows to gather more wisdom, and we include our Soul Family.

The Akashic Record Keepers have shared with me that the soul is so vast, it doesn't fit into a human body on Earth or in many other worlds, so the soul has chosen to split into aspects of the Larger Oversoul. These aspects of your souls having different life experiences continue to evolve. Over a tremendous amount of time, billions of our years, the original soul appears to be multiplying.

The Record Keepers explain that there is never one aspect of us living life. There can be millions of us living millions of lives. We are connected to our Oversoul, receiving all the information and wisdom we gain through our various lifetimes. I find it challenging to grasp the idea that, without space and time, everything happens simultaneously in the Quantum Field of Source.

Over the millennia, we continue to break into more aspects of the soul, living more lives on Earth and in many other dimensions or worlds. Since the soul has now lived and continues to live numerous lifetimes, those original twenty-five souls in your soul's family (the people inside the elevator, from the parable) eventually become hundreds or thousands of family members who are available to support you when they are needed.

Our Oversoul has cumulative soul experiences adding up to thousands of lifetimes on Earth and in other worlds and dimensions. As a result, we develop many soul contracts outside of our original Soul Family. The worldly experiences and any karma we create from these additional contracts help us learn and evolve as a soul.

We are also more inclusive when in soul form than you may imagine. We often adopt souls and bring them into our soul group to help them progress. For example, you might find you have a contract with someone who seems like a very young soul. It could be that you wrote an agreement to support them in their progression as they learn here on Earth.

Why is My Relationship So Challenging?

So often, my clients will ask, "Why would I pick this challenging life filled with survival issues and trauma?"

When we experience challenges that cause mental, emotional, or physical trauma, they are part of the growth our soul desires. They present opportunities to evolve in love and wisdom. We can write our soul contracts to include karma, which means there is an old story that we are still stuck in. When we stay stuck, believing it's someone else's fault, we can't move forward, and our soul doesn't grow. Like a hamster's wheel, stuck karma keeps us going around and we can't figure out how to get off. The more we spin, the more frustrated we get.

Your soul wants to understand the challenge so you can choose to act in a new and different way. For example, when driving your car, you might decide to take another road next time! In looking at our situations, whether challenging or not, we can see new possibilities. As you face your challenges, remember that your soul wants to learn how to overcome the traumas and issues that stand between you and more joy. You can create a good life filled with love. But first, you must overcome what stands in your way.

When we move from feeling like a victim in our life to understanding that we chose these experiences, our infinite souls become empowered.

The Primary Reason a Soul Comes to Earth

Please remember that the primary reason a soul comes to Earth is to learn and grow, and that our tiny bodies do not represent the vast souls we are in truth. Your soul also comes to this beautiful planet to experience and enjoy all life has to offer.

The Akashic Record Keepers often remind us that we are here to be of service. It is another one of our reasons for this experience. The Record Keepers are here to provide information about our soul's plan and our greater truth. The expansive view and information from the records can assist us in moving out of the emotional pain and chaos that this dimension often causes.

The mantra below will remind you of your soul's truth. Take a moment to put your hand over your heart, close your eyes, and take a deep breath as you say to yourself:

I am an infinite soul, having this human experience. I grow and awaken with ease and grace. All is in the perfect Divine right order.

Repeat at least three times in a row or continually, as a mantra, if you are under stress. It may be beneficial to repeat often, to remember who you are as an infinite soul.

My Thoughts on Life Challenges

After my two best friends died while we were in school, I felt abandoned by them. I also felt like a failure because I couldn't save them. I felt unworthy of having been the one who lived. Why did I survive? And why did they die?

My ego told me I couldn't help them and that they had left me. For a brief time after each of these traumas, I decided to throw in the towel on life. I gave up looking for answers in my spiritual quests because none of my studying, reading spiritual books, and taking philosophy classes helped me. I slid into an unworthy pattern, as many of us do during traumatic periods in our lives.

My constant thought was that if I wasn't able to save them, then I was unworthy to go on to fulfill my soul plan as a healer. I was angry at God for taking my teenage soul sisters from me. I found myself blaming God as well as myself. But, at that point, it never dawned on me that their deaths had nothing to do with me. I was grieving too much to see clearly what their souls had planned. My heart was too broken to see beyond my pain.

We are often egocentric and believe that everything is about us. However, my years of talking to the Akashic Masters have taught me that each soul has its own plan, which includes support for others and learning from our many relationships. We still make choices based on our free will, but eventually, we return to our soul's plan to learn and develop more compassion and love.

As a traumatized, abandoned, and angry nineteen-year-old, I decided that my punishment was to give up my esoteric beliefs and just be human. No more searching for my galactic home and higher meaning. Instead, I chose to do—whatever it is humans do. I decided to place my more heightened conscious awareness and all the gifts I'd come to share into an imaginary shoebox. I hid it away, high up on an etheric shelf, for years to come.

Many of you might have done something similar. Maybe you didn't tuck your gifts and memories of who you were into a shoebox like I did; maybe you did something more dramatic. Possibly, when you were little, you were conscious of the incredible expanse of the cosmos, but then life beat you down. Did you see and talk to angels or fairies? What about family members who had passed away? Did they visit you to offer their love?

Maybe you had unloving, distant, or cold parents—not because they didn't love you, but because they didn't know how to love. They were likely victims of abusive parents themselves and continued to be emotionally traumatized. To your child-self, feeling unloved can lead to feeling of being unworthy in life. We label ourselves inadequate because we didn't receive the love we wanted and needed. These are all false thoughts and beliefs. These ideas are not valid from the soul's perspective found in your Akashic Record.

Your Akashic Record gives you a more comprehensive picture of what is going on to help facilitate the lessons you want to learn more quickly. Some of our growth comes from challenging relationships and the connected traumas.

The Record Keepers explain the different kinds of soul contracts you may have with your family. You might discover a surprising truth: your parents are not always the central part of your soul contracts! Sometimes, we contract with a sibling, aunt, grandparent, or even a family friend, to be our supporter. They are not biological parents, but they are just as important for our journey.

Possibly, your parents agreed in your soul plan to deny you what you think you needed, so you would dare to stand in your truth and empowerment. You might then grow up to teach others to do the same, which was part of the plan. You might do this as a high school teacher, a parent, or a team leader in a business. There are no set ways for us to use our gifts. Free will is involved.

The universe is never heedless. Your traumas and challenges will lead to something more significant in your life as long as you are open to the lessons and gifts they may bring. The biggest challenge in being a human is that we have been programmed by the collective mind to think and feel like victims. We habitually feel we've been punished or are unworthy of love and all the good of the world. We rarely see it as our highest soul plan to fulfill our soul's desires.

Please don't underestimate yourself and the power of your soul's plan. We are complex and ancient souls looking to evolve. Give yourself the gift of continually expanding your experiences. Go outside of what you usually think your life purpose is, and look more deeply into your challenges. Look for the truth.

Soul Contract with Groups

There is so much change going on with Earth and all its inhabitants. Significant contracts are being activated to help humanity change by transforming the old paradigms in the collective programming that have been in place for the last 9,000 years. Think of women's rights, culture and race, sex, and gender rights. These massive contracts require millions of souls around the globe to transform the old energy into something new.

Millions are needed to heal our beautiful Mother Earth and support humanity to awaken. Massive soul group contracts are in place to end abuse of all kinds: physical, emotional, sexual, and mental. Hundreds of thousands of souls are embodied on the planet right now to help balance the male and female energy, which has been out of balance for more than 4,000 years. We see gender inequality in many ways, including in relationships, unequal salaries, gender discrimination in education, sexual violence, and lack of bodily autonomy.

How Are the Contracts Written?

When souls decide to come to Earth, their plan starts to evolve. But first, they choose why they incarnate on Earth and what they will do with their time here. Then they decide how they wish to help humanity. For most of us, healing our karmic patterns left over from past lives will ensure soul growth for the person and collective healing for humanity.

A soul plan can feel overwhelming when you have a big task to accomplish. However, the Akashic Masters assure us that all Akashic Record Keepers are in service to us. We can use their guidance to take baby steps as we come to understand our relationships and their challenges. They will help us grow into the consciousness necessary to fulfill our plan.

If you are part of the soul group that is here to end abuse on our planet, you might have chosen to be part of a family or relationship where you experience one or more types of abuse. But remember, you are working on your own past life and personal karma around abuse as well as supporting a shift in humanity.

In the next chapter, we'll go into greater depth about soul contracts with karma.

EXERCISE FOR REFLECTION

1. Were you born into a family that told you that you live in a fantasy world, always making stuff up? Did they call you crazy?

2. Did the people who raised you say you were stupid because school wasn't your strong suit?

3. Have you ever thought: Why was I born into this family?

Below are powerful prayers to release the stuck emotions relating to your family and soul family karmic connections. Use them until you feel an energetic release.

PRAYER FOR HEALING FAMILY RELATIONSHIPS

Mother, Father, Goddess, God, I give great thanks for the blessings of my family of origin and the family that raised me. I acknowledge and release any judgments I have of them and I send them pure, unconditional love.

We are all Divine souls on a journey, and I bless you with your journey as I go on my way, following my own Soul Path.

So it is. Blessed Be.

PRAYER FOR HEALING ABUSE

Mother, Father, Goddess, God, I am filled with the Divine light, and my soul connects more deeply into my body as I acknowledge this truth.

I know the trauma and pain I have experienced on many levels in this life, and I now choose to release the pain from every cell in my body.

I walk away from the old story and choose a new path to happiness.

I know the people involved in my story are truly Divine souls at their core, and I can now move into my heart and feel a pure level of forgiveness for them.

As I release the painful emotions, I see the memories that arise and I bless them and send them on their way.

They are no longer my truth.

I go on my way, following my soul path filled with the love of the Divine.

So it is. Blessed Be.

PRAYER FOR WORTHINESS OF UNIQUE SELF

Mother, Father, Goddess, God, I claim my uniqueness and liberate the collective consciousness that has held me in constraint.

I am free of all holds that seized my self-worth.

I step away from the desire for public approval.

I release the group contracts and agreements that no longer serve my highest good and move beyond the limitations of authority.

I am worthy of expressing myself as my God-self and doing so now and each day forward.

I claim this truth for myself and all I meet.

So it is. Blessed Be.

In the next chapter, we will start the journey of karma and karmic lessons.

CHAPTER 4

COMPLETED KARMA = SOUL GROWTH

O ur reality is far vaster than our mind is capable of understanding. Your commitment to learning about and working through old karmic patterns can create an energetic opening for more abundance in your life. I believe karma is misunderstood, so I want to expand your understanding of this concept.

Consider karma as a tool for learning and growing on a soul level—not as a punishment or something to fear. Karma can take lifetimes to complete, or it can happen immediately, in some instances. For example, the karmic patterns around emotional trauma, abuse, or betrayal must be worked on in layers, and might take many lifetimes to heal and clear.

Throughout this chapter, I will share examples of karmic patterns. These are real-life scenarios of clients' karmic lessons discovered in their Akashic Record consultations. They had energy blocks from these karmic lessons, which we were able to release in their session. Removing the blocks helps my clients move on in their relationships with themselves and others. You may find your own life reflected in some of the examples.

As your understanding of karmic lessons and soul growth expands, you will know what karma is and isn't, and where to find it in your relationships with money, work, and family. It's an adventure—but so well worth it!

What Karma is Not

Karma works in many different ways. But contrary to what many people think, it is not a punishment for something they have done and it does not cause bad things to happen to them. That is just not true.

There are Quick and Clear-Cut Karmic Lessons

Most of us have some quick, micro-karmic daily lessons that offer us insight to either slow down, be more understanding, or forgive ourselves. Some demonstrate we are over-extended energetically.

This example is a very common, quick, micro-karmic lesson you might not pick up on: You are running late to work, in a hurry, and you find yourself behind a slow driver. Frustrated, you swerve around them, cutting someone off whom you didn't see because you weren't looking. Horns blow and swearing happens with a few hand gestures; now you are outraged. You finally make it to the parking lot of work and you are about to pull into a parking space when another car comes out of nowhere, cutting you off and taking your parking space.

That is an example of short and clear-cut karma coming back to you. What do you think the lesson might have been?

This example might also teach a more important lesson. Maybe it's a wake-up call to calm down and be patient. Perhaps you are moving too quickly and unconsciously in your life. You could have an accident, hurting yourself or others. Think about it and you'll see that many other scenarios could have occurred. Losing a parking space might be the least disruptive karmic lesson in your day. However, if you continue to be angry at the person who stole your parking space, the karmic lesson will not be so quick and easy. It's always your choice.

Even quick and clear-cut karmic lessons can teach powerful, in-the-moment life lessons that can change our attitudes in many ways, if we let them. Many of our life lessons are simple, yet profound. When we move through life consciously, we can feel less stressed and more energetic. We can release the worry that has been depleting us.

How Simple Karmic Lessons Become Big Ones

A quick karmic lesson while driving a car can save you from an accident, which would be a much bigger karmic call to action. But if you don't get the quick and easy message, the calls will get louder to get your attention until you stop, discover, and let go of the karmic pattern that is no longer necessary.

Hitting a Brick Wall Demolished a Karmic Lesson

How often do we use "hitting a brick wall" as a symbolic statement in telling a story? Well, for one of my clients, it was a literal statement. Luckily, no one was hurt—other than her pocketbook. It was a time in Julie's life when she had the rug pulled out from under her because of over-giving to family members and under-giving to herself. Before that moment, life had been great, from her point of view.

One morning, after months in survival mode, emotionally, mentally, and spiritually, she inadvertently stepped on the accelerator instead of the brake when pulling into her parking space. As a result, she hit a brick wall just a couple of feet in front of her. Julie told me that she felt like she was in a dream when it was happening. It seemed the whole scenario had a life of its own. She knew her soul was waking her up, but she did not know why.

Julie had spent months in the traumatic experience, not understanding why she hit a brick wall with her car. When she reached out for an Akashic consultation, she learned of an old karmic pattern of "doing too much for others to ensure she would receive love." There was still an old, relentless "unworthiness" karmic pattern in her that kept repeating.

After our work together, she slowly withdrew from her survival mode of doing everything for others and not for herself. This karmic pattern had engulfed all areas of her life in both obvious and subtle ways. By letting go, Julie had more energy and felt safer making choices to take care of herself first.

Julie had experienced a few quick and clear-cut reminders about a possible karmic lesson, but she hadn't been willing to look at them. Her survival mode around worthiness has been too strong. It literally took "hitting a brick wall" to wake her up.

Souls Lessons from Survival Mode

When we were born, our most important mission was to survive. Our soul had a reason for being here; therefore, it tried to make sure our parents or caretakers would care for our basic human needs. We needed enough food and to stay safe, and we had the human need for love. Depending on the life lessons we chose, our soul's initial mission to survive would either be fulfilled or not, depending on the contracts it made with other souls and whether they held up their side of the contract.

If only we were aware of our soul's plan, we could follow it without any detours or fears. Yet most of us stumble through life lessons. Being in survival mode is the most significant detour when striving for our life's purpose. Our survival instincts can create havoc with our goals and dreams if we become locked in negative thoughts and emotions.

Some people grow up in dangerous parts of the world or in a home with abusive people. They make survival their main focus in life, both consciously and unconsciously. Many of us who didn't live that kind of life are mainly focused on survival, too. The soul uses the lens of survival to help us discover old karmic lessons we will need to heal to reach our life purpose.

As we become aware of how we are repeating survival patterns, we can start to let go of them. It's easier once we understand that these are not life-or-death situations. We can then consciously begin to risk making new choices by trusting that our soul has a plan to help us reach our life purpose.

The Soul Uses Trust or Our Lack of It

Learning to trust is a challenge for most of us because we feel too vulnerable. When alone, we can feel powerless. The soul uses our lack of trust for its growth. Imagine many of our lifetimes filled with trauma, tragedy, and betrayal, which makes the karmic lesson of trust feel like much more of a risk. But we must risk taking a chance to trust ourselves, our God, and others. It is human nature to fear anything new and different; many won't take the riskier path because of this fear. And that is okay. There is no right or wrong answer with soul work.

Learning from and eventually overcoming karma surrounding trusting isn't easy, but it's worth the work to have the freedom to make new choices. Your ancient soul gets to share its light, wisdom, and love to affect those around you, whether the effect is subtle or dramatic.

We often don't know when we are doing the soul's work in finishing a contract or karma. Not every situation is traumatic, as you read in my examples. As ancient and wise souls, we have all come so that, in our own unique way, we can change the outcome of the planet's trajectory to create a new Heaven on Earth.

You Are an Ancient Soul

Just think about it: You might have had lifetimes in Egypt in 3000 B.C.; Africa in 2500 B.C.; or Persia in 550 B.C. That would make you ancient, wouldn't it?

We've all lived in various places at different times. However, in all of the Akashic Records work I've done through the years, I have rarely met someone who has lived on Earth for fewer than 200 lifetimes. Because we are ancient souls, there are many layers to the karma we choose in each lifetime, depending on the life purposes we chose. I found it interesting that most of us interested in spirituality—and most significantly, in the Akashic Records— have lived at least 400 lives on Earth. Just imagine all the karmic lessons that need healing to move into the amount of trust we need to believe in a higher power.

Uncovering Soul Gifts

If we write our own soul plan, why would we pick a challenging lifetime? Not an easy question to answer. The reasons are complex, just as we are complex souls. One of the many answers is karma. We use karma from past lifetimes to course-correct different relationships with ourselves, the planet, and others. Our soul wants to experience every possible facet and outcome and, in doing so, we create karma. These are also called karmic patterns. Buddhists refer to the Karmic Wheel of Life. Remember, karma is neither good nor bad; it is about learning, healing, and growing.

The Akashic Record Keepers tell us that we have been caught in a loop, or on a karmic wheel, for thousands of years with many karmic issues and patterns that keep running repeatedly. Our reason for being here is to break these karmic patterns. Then we can transform that energy, which will unlock our gifts. This work will be vital to fulfilling our soul's purpose.

My work has led me to recognize most of humanity struggles. We have challenging families, work at jobs we hate, and juggle numerous relationships. Some feel stuck in a loveless marriage because they believe they can't afford to leave. Suppose they could take a step back to see that they are stuck in survival mode. Then, they might slowly move away from what isn't working to align with their soul's plan and reveal its gifts.

Humanity has challenges because we are rebalancing the ancient karmic patterns of deeply engrained patriarchal belief systems passed on through generations in many families, societies, religions, and cultures. But unfortunately, the struggle in working to change this male/female imbalance has created much chaos and friction. For thousands of years, women were repressed, becoming enslaved people, prostitutes, and chattel owned by men. Many lightworkers are here now to uncover their unique gifts and help end abuse by balancing feminine/masculine power and awakening other souls to their light and love.

Record Keepers Shared with Me

Dear Ones,

It is everyone's purpose to rebalance the two most vital energies, male and female, on the planet. Without balance, the power of the male energy will overrun humanity, including our dear Mother Earth. If she succumbs to pollution and global warming, everyone will die. Mother Earth will not perish, but it will take hundreds, maybe thousands, of years to recover. Of course, your souls will go on into other dimensions and realms, yet the karmic patterns may continue in different ways. Please stay vigilant and aware of your actions and do all you can to assist with healing Gaia.

Dear Ones,

Remember that when you raise your vibrational field through meditation or learning to access your Akashic Records, including utilizing many other healing tools too numerous to mention, you are helping humanity shift. Your life's purpose is to raise humanity out of the old, lower vibrational timeline to move into a more positive, higher frequency timeline where you will thrive instead of dying. Overcoming the challenging karmic lessons is a big part of it all.

EXERCISE FOR REFLECTION

1. What changes in your life would you want to see if you consciously released your unconscious karma?

2. In which areas of your life do you feel you have unfinished karma?

3. Name the area of your life you will work on first.

Forgiveness is a powerful tool to clear karma. Is there someone you can start forgiving to release old karma?

PRAYER OF FORGIVENESS

Divine, Spirit, Source, please move me into a state of forgiveness toward anyone or anything that has hurt me, consciously or unconsciously, from the beginning of time to this present moment. I now forgive them, and I release the energy of the past.

Divine, Spirit, Source, please move me into a state of forgiveness toward myself for any hurt I have caused others, consciously or unconsciously, from the beginning of time to this present moment. I now forgive myself, and I release the energy of the past.

Divine, Spirit, Source, please move me into a state of forgiveness for any hurt I have caused myself, consciously or unconsciously, from the beginning of time to this present moment. I now forgive myself and release the energy of the past.

I invoke the grace and power of forgiveness to transform my body, mind, and heart as I return to a state of Divine Innocence.

And so it is. Blessed Be. Amen.

PRAYER FOR RELEASING BLAME

Mother, Father, Goddess, God, help me to grow so that I can comfortably take responsibility for my actions and my life.

I understand that I AM a Creator Being having a human experience.

I release old blame and belief that anyone has "done this to me."

I stand in my power as a Divine Creator of my life experience.

So it is. Blessed Be.

PRAYER TO FREE YOURSELF FROM RESENTMENT

Mother, Father, Goddess, God, please bring me to consciousness about the ill will I have created toward others.

I ask to understand the greater wisdom so I may replace this resentment and anger with love.

As I make this shift within myself, I know we all move into a higher alignment.

So it is. Blessed Be.

Now that you have learned about your karma, it's time to dive into your talents and gifts.

CHAPTER 5

TALENTS AND GIFTS = PURPOSE

Most of us wonder about our soul's purpose or life path. Unfortunately, our questions lead to nonspecific answers, confusion, and frustration. Aren't you glad to know, without a doubt, that your soul created a plan—and you get to discover it? Life is a journey!

The Akashic Record Keepers explain that we are complicated souls and that we bring gifts and talents to use for our soul's purpose with each lifetime. We must discover and develop these talents and skills so we can wield them with precision. Unfortunately, we often have no idea which talents we have or how or when they will show up.

After fifteen years of sliding down an unlikely path into the human side of life, far from my own path, I realized I was sick. I found that I had chronic fatigue syndrome. I worked with a talented acupuncturist who slowly helped me to heal. It took years. I didn't realize it then, but now it is so apparent: My soul's purpose was to be a healer. Not understanding the path I was to follow, I discovered and trained in numerous modalities, searching for the "right" fit. And then, the Akashic Masters came into my life.

When the Akashic Masters Came to Me

I was doing intuitive readings and energy healings for my clients when something happened that changed my life. Occasionally, the information I received was very different, more profound, and more expansive. Years later, I learned I had received this profound guidance from my clients' Akashic Records. These messages came from the beings of light who kept their Akashic Records. I wanted to know more about this energy field and its insightful information. Because of my desire to learn more, they found me.

Through a twist of fate, I met a woman who told me that the extensive information I received came from Akashic Records. My original energy healing teacher had taught me about the Akashic Field, but she'd said, "No one is allowed to go in. You only go to the gates of the Akashic Library and ask for energy healing for your clients."

So, for many years, I would go to the gates of the Akashic Records to ask for energy to help heal my client. I could see the energy come down and fill their body, but I never spoke to the beings behind the gate.

Eventually, I was shown how to access these extensive libraries of information consciously and deliberately. Finally, the door was opened, and I could access the soul's Akashic Records, which I have been doing ever since.

One day, the Akashic Record Keepers asked me to start a school teaching others how to access and gain information from their own soul's records. They reminded me that, with the dawn of the Age of Aquarius, it was time to help humanity become empowered by accessing their soul's wisdom and guidance.

Their challenge seemed daunting; even so, I followed their guidance, step by step, and have never looked back. The Record

Keepers have been there for me every bit of the way. They have put people in my path who would assist me on the way forward, open doors to grow my student body, and guide all of my work. The blessings became numerous when I chose to align with the work my soul had planned for me so many eons ago. The third book, which you have in your hands, was given to me by them, which is just one more example of their loving guidance.

After years of doing Akashic Readings and Healings for clients and teaching students worldwide, it was time to download my own Akashic Access Keys and start the Akashic Knowing School of Wisdom. We now have eight Sacred Access Keys to assist all the Starseeds in quickly accessing their own Akasha.

Over the years, I have trained thousands of students worldwide with the technology of the internet and online teaching platforms. I also have certified dozens of students as Akashic Consultants and Akashic Record Teachers. I continue to expand the work through radio, summits, books, Akashic Business courses, and Mastery courses. The record keepers guide me to more work, and I keep stepping into it with their help.

When my dear friends died while I was in high school, I felt abandoned and mortified at the idea of continuing my life alone. I had no idea this would be my future. It seemed unlikely that I would be writing this book now and that my soul had a big plan I could accomplish with love, integrity, and much support. But although I didn't know it, I was on a path to discover and uncover my gifts and talents to fulfill my soul's work. The most empowering lesson they ever taught me was to never to judge myself or my journey.

The Akashic Record Keepers have become my best friends, daily companions, and trusted guides. They came through with support, unconditional love, and wisdom when they started talking to me. At first, I didn't know it was them. The information they shared went from past lives to present soul contracts and sometimes into the future. It was more wisdom and guidance than I had ever received intuitively. All of it just wowed me.

The beauty of accessing my personal Akashic Record Keepers is that I have the privilege to ask them questions daily. I started asking them my most heartfelt questions.

What did I return to do?

They would tell me: *To help bring the Akashic Field back to Earth.*

I told them, *But I'm a suburban mom with three small children. Why would you pick me?* Their answer shook my world.

Akashic Masters answered:

Because you were one of Us. You started your soul's journey as an Akashic Record Keeper. You eventually went on your way to becoming a creator being, helping to create worlds.

You have held the Akashic vibration for millennia as a Record Keeper for humanity. Now it is time to connect this higher vibration back to Earth so people can easily access it. We request your assistance in this task. We are calling on all the ancient Record Keepers to help, but many do not hear our call. Some feel unworthy or afraid to be seen, as they have been killed many times for speaking out about spirituality.

They also shared with me:

We have entered a new age, a new astrological alignment, and a New Age referred to as a Yuga in Sanskrit. It is time to upgrade the world and reconnect with the Akasha field. People abused the Akashic Field in the Dark Ages and were denied access for many years. They used the information in evil ways for personal and political gain. For example, many used the Akashic Field to find secrets to rob, steal, and pillage. They would target people to discover where they stored their gold and gems. Generals asked for battle strategies to win the war against their enemies.

Humans have a way of abusing power, and humans found a lot of information in the Akashic Records to abuse. So the Akashic Record Keepers removed its higher vibration from Earth. The only humans with the ability to continue accessing the field of energy were the mystics, shamans, and awakened people, and that was because they went through rigorous training for years. This lack of access to the Akashic Field lasted for one thousand years.

I had never heard this information explained. It was fascinating to finally make sense of what my first psychic teacher had taught me: that we could go up to the gates of the Akashic Records to ask for healing energy for our clients, but we were never allowed to go in.

At the end of every intuitive healing, I could see sparkling energy, books, quills, waterfalls, and other magnificent symbols entering my client's crown chakra. It took me five years to realize that the Record Keepers gave my clients the information and healing energy through me. Then, my teachers taught me that the Akashic Records and the Record Keepers were off-limits. But much to my surprise, they spoke to me—and they have been talking ever since.

That was an exciting learning moment for me. Please don't always believe what your teachers tell you. Ask within your own heart: *Does this feel true for me?* All teachers, myself included, are human and can be misinformed.

The Akashic Field Opened to Humanity

I want you to know that, after one thousand years, there has been another shift in the energetic alignment. The Akashic Field has been opened up to humanity again. The Record Keepers wish our assistance in spreading the word that extensive information and healing energy are accessible to us now. All who seek to work in the Akashic Records will have the ability to understand the Soul's Plan and receive guidance.

The only way to change the world is for thousands of us to carry more light. How do we do that? By overcoming our karmic patterns to uncover our gifts and talents. We can use compassion and forgiveness for ourselves and others to speed up the process. The grace we receive from forgiveness allows us to be the love so many need at this time. All we have to do is hold the energy of love in our hearts and we can raise the vibration globally. Easy, right?

These simple acts will allow humanity to continue without a world war or major catastrophe. Please do not underestimate the power of your light. And remember, no matter where you are in your life, being of service to humanity means using compassion and love everywhere: at work, with your family and friends, or as you are raising your kids. When you smile at others, you are sharing light.

It Started with Small and Meaningful Intentions

Our twin daughters were born when my son was only eighteen months old. I had little time or energy to do anything significant for humanity. I decided I could set an intention to live with love in my heart, and to feel that love wherever I went. I also became a Religious Science Prayer Practitioner to participate in prayer healing for the congregation. I shared energy healing with my friends and family, and I loved my babies with all my heart. I sent them big love and saw the good in them, so they could see it in themselves as they grew up. According to the Record Keepers, my instincts were enough, as an open and loving heart vibrates into the world.

Clients often ask me about their soul's purpose because they feel they haven't done enough. Yet it's common for these clients to be nurses, engineers, and tech people, all doing service work in many ways. One of the great blessings of having a conversation with your Record Keepers is you can learn that you're not wasting time or messing up. They explain that our path to our soul's purpose is complex, and not one is the same. There are many paths to the mountain top, and each one reaches the quantum field of Source.

For too long, I felt like I was wasting time because of my anger over the deaths of my two dear friends. That led me down a different path than I had expected to be on in my twenties. I was spiritually aware, but it didn't matter, as I made a break with my spiritual path. My path was anything but spiritually aware in the 1970s while living in San Francisco. My spiritual life never crossed my mind until my anger and misdirection turned into a serious illness, which prompted a course correction.

When I was home with my children, I asked the Record Keepers if I'd messed up my life and missed my big chance at enlightenment. I was one of those weird kids who had thought about enlightenment as far back as fourteen years old. The Record Keepers laughed in their pure, unconditional love as they told me: *Of course not! All those experiences in your twenties paved the path to help you discover your greatest gifts of compassion and non-judgment.*

This answer was a huge relief. I had been so hard on myself, thinking I'd blown my chance to help humanity and become enlightened. But what they told me made sense, because my experiences had taught me never to judge anyone or their path. After all, one doesn't know how or when they will discover their talents and gifts.

The knowledge they shared also helped with my parenting. Even my children's friends mentioned how much love and support they felt from me. I know from personal experience that it's not easy to be a teenager, as I remember being that age so clearly. However, loving our children unconditionally is a perfect antidote. *Unconditionally* doesn't mean we allow them to be irresponsible, out of control, or without boundaries; it means loving them through their karmic lessons, so that they may discover their talents and gifts.

Baby steps. That's what walking my path has been like over my lifetime. But when I think of where I've landed, something new always arises, and my baby steps lead me to ask more questions to learn more about the extended world around us.

Your Gifts Create a Beautiful Pearl Necklace

Let's explore how different lifetimes can accumulate the gifts you need in this one. First, imagine a life when you've loved your work and lived with purpose and fulfillment. You were an author who wrote and published many popular books in that lifetime. Now imagine that this lifetime represents a beautiful pearl on the etheric plane.

Fast forward to another lifetime, a few hundred years later, when you had a similar life, but you were a poet this time. Your poems were about love, which opened the hearts of your admirers and taught people about love. Now imagine that this life represents another beautiful pearl on the etheric plane.

Now let's go back 2300 years, to a lifetime when you were a scribe in the great library of Alexandria, which was a significant job and highly regarded. Now imagine the etheric plane; that lifetime represents another beautiful pearl.

You were a monk laboring over copying the Bible in beautiful calligraphy with decorative borders in a different lifetime. Your work was revered for its beauty and accuracy. On the etheric plane, imagine that life as another beautiful pearl.

Now see your four beautiful pearls strung together in a necklace. In your next lifetime, you decide to utilize the pearl of the writer as one of the talents you bring to Earth.

In that lifetime, you become a communicator of the spoken word by publishing books and speaking on stages. Your pearl necklace, filled with the experiences and trade skills of being a successful scribe and author, will assist you in fulfilling your work.

Another example is using talents from multiple lifetimes

to fulfill your soul's plan. You have many pearl necklaces in the etheric plane to utilize in other lifetimes. You decide to incarnate with a large group of souls contracted to balance masculine and feminine energy. You will use pearls from two lifetimes when you were a high priestess. Each one helped you develop unique talents. In one, you were a woman caring for street children, and in another, you were a Divine wise woman in a temple in India. Being a high priestess offered you the gifts and talents of the awakened seer, which you can use to facilitate your purpose of supporting humanity in this incarnation.

Your necklace symbolizes all the talents, gifts, and training you carry for your purpose. Your gifts become intertwined with those of other souls, to be used in unison as all of you fulfill a higher purpose.

Another way you use the seer gifts is to help people discover the imbalance of male/female energy in different settings and learn how to balance it. For example, the imbalance shows when you work in a corporate environment where male energies are predominant. Your career places you in the corporate field as, let's say, an attorney. The soul plan considers where your gifts and talents can create the most significant impact. So you are placed there to help balance the male and female energies. In addition, your soul may have put you there to create a shift in salaries, so that men and women are paid equally.

Counseling couples can also reveal your purpose to balance energies, as you help them balance the masculine and feminine energies in their relationship and family. Or you might choose to work with women, helping them overcome their fear of stepping more fully into their feminine power and unconditional love.

You might be helping other women hold the sacred Divine Feminine and have a group contract to help balance the planet's masculine/feminine energies. In this lifetime, you might have contracted to have a loving and supportive partner, so that you could create a business around helping to bring balance to men and women through authoring books and speaking at corporations.

Another possibility: Your seer gifts might enable you to start a women's healing circle, providing an opportunity for many soul sisters from past lives to gather to support each other in their journey. The seer's gifts give you the clairvoyant and intuitive nature that allows you to do readings for your healing circle. Now you are fully living out your soul's plan. The pearls you have gathered in the many lifetimes become recycled as the world evolves.

Many of you are lightworkers here to raise the vibration of humanity. Your role might be as a mom, a bank manager, or in a corporate office. You'll find so many other jobs, careers, or business choices that also support your plan.

These examples show essential parts of the work we do to raise the frequency of the world, so that humanity will have more love and compassion for each other. And your role can show up in so many ways. But, most importantly, your purpose in your job/career/business is to hold a higher vibration and to support any healing energy needed. In doing so, you begin to see that, whatever you do and with whomever you are doing it, there is a greater purpose—your soul's purpose.

EXERCISE FOR REFLECTION

1. How can you expand your idea about your job or the career path you've chosen?

2. How can you use your talents to be of service to yourself, your family, and your community?

3. Is there something you are being gently guided to do in your life?

Remember: No job is too small to add the soul's desire to serve humanity in its unique way. No matter what you do or where you are on your path, you are serving. Remember to smile and give plenty of heart to those around you.

PRAYER TO ALIGN WITH DHARMA

Mother, Father, Goddess, God, I am centered in my body as I align my mind, spirit, and body with my soul purpose and Dharma.

I embrace the unique soul as I embody my soul gifts.

I incorporate a consistent spiritual practice in my life.

I am of service to my family and community in ways that align with my light.

I am grateful for the ease in which love and grace flow through my life.

So it is. Blessed Be.

I used this prayer to feel and experience being of service. I read it three times a day for fourteen days. Within that timeframe, I was contacted for help by numerous people, and I'm now working with those individuals. I've immersed myself in the purpose of my soul. Thank You, God. I am blessed.

PRAYER TO BE OF SERVICE

Mother, Father, Goddess, God, I am blessed to be a soul of service.

Please help me to know the highest and best work I can do for myself, my family, and my community today.

So it is. Blessed Be.

PRAYER OF SELF-VALUING

Mother, Father, Goddess, God, please support me as I step into my knowing of the truth of myself as a Divine soul.

Please connect me to this expansive memory and align me with the knowledge of how I came to be of service.

I treasure myself as an ancient and infinite soul.

I cherish the gifts I have to offer humanity.

I share them with humility and grace.

So It Is. Blessed Be.

In the next chapter, we will discover how past lives offer wisdom for today.

CHAPTER 6

PAST LIVES
= WISDOM

Have you lived more than one life?

Reincarnation has been the subject of so much speculation. Is this life really our only chance to get it right? Wouldn't you love to find out that you can do it over again, knowing that you take with you what you have learned in this life?

The Record Keepers say that we live thousands of lives, hundreds on Earth and thousands in other realms and dimensions. As we travel, as infinite souls, our soul families expand. We learn, grow, and enjoy life in a body here on Earth. There are so many senses to experience, a cornucopia of places, people, ideas, thoughts, beliefs, and feelings.

Have you ever met a new acquaintance who feels very familiar, as though you have been in each other's lives for years? On the other hand, there may be an individual you feel intense anger toward, even though you just met. Or you meet a person that you know is "the one" the first time you meet.

Can these encounters really be random? I don't believe they are, and everything I know and have learned from the Akashic

Record Keepers over the last thirty years assures me that life is not random. We do reincarnate with a soul plan and soul families.

Let me ask you: Have you ever visited a new place only to discover you know your way around? Who have you met for the first time in your life that you felt deeply connected to? How often have you dreamed of living in another place or on another planet?

Is Reincarnation Real?

Different religious perspectives and teachings only add to the confusion with their diverse speculation as to whether we have lived lifetimes before this one. From all the spiritual teachings I've studied throughout the years, it still doesn't make any sense to me that our soul would only create one life. In that one life, you would have to make a choice that would affect your eternal life. How could you have acquired enough wisdom, knowledge, and gifts in just one life to make an educated decision?

I have often contemplated the lack of fairness in only living one life. Imagine all of the diversity in the world, including all the cultures, socioeconomics, health or wealth possibilities, race, gender, and so many more options. Why is one person so poor that they live on the street and die of hunger and disease when another person is born into a wealthy family with endless possibilities? Then, according to many religions, both souls are judged the same for their actions.

The Akashic Record Keepers explain that we come to Earth to experience every kind of life situation, even the painful ones. It's possible that you lived in luxury in one life, not considering the less fortunate people around you. In another incarnation, you wanted to experience life without the basic necessities. You might come back to help balance the inequalities in your world, using what you learned during those two lifetimes. You could work in government, or as a philanthropist, or in any number of careers where you could support greater equality.

We experience many facets of life through reincarnation. We return to help humanity with the wisdom we've learned from our previous lifetimes.

Some Ancient Religions Teach Reincarnation

When I minored in philosophy at Humboldt State University, I was fascinated by Hinduism and Buddhism. These religions believe in reincarnation and validate the innate wisdom I was aware of from childhood.

Hinduism is one of the oldest religions and it is the world's third largest religion, with a billion followers worldwide. According to Hindu tradition, death is not the end of a person's soul. They believe the soul continues to reincarnate based on the actions of the soul in their life on Earth. Positive actions will support progress in the evolution of the soul, where negative, or selfish acts may lead to the soul reborn as an animal. This continuing cycle of life and rebirth will eventually lead to salvation and reuniting with the Divine dharma. It is regarded in Hinduism as a cosmic law underlying right behavior and social order and in Buddhism, the nature of reality regarded as a universal truth taught by the Buddha. An aspect of truth or reality is to live in alignment as a moral and righteous person. When we live our dharma, in Divine order, we are not creating more karma. A simple way to look at your dharma is as your Divine purpose while karma is the universe's way of telling you when you stray from the path of your dharma.

The ultimate salvation, called *Moksha,* is when the soul unites with Creator and is free of the life-and-death cycle.

Buddhism teaches the idea of reincarnation also. Buddhists believe that each new life builds on the past life. They also believe that, if you do not live a selfless life, you will be reborn as an animal. In this modern time, there is less belief in rebirth as an animal and a greater belief in karma, meaning your next life, good or challenging, is based on your past actions. Rebirth can take place in six realms and is not always on Earth. As in Hinduism, the soul continues to learn and be reborn until the soul is free from desire and reaches a state of oneness with the universe.

Followers of Hinduism believe in the ideas of free will and choice. Though its followers might not feel they have chosen to be born into a dysfunctional family or with a health challenge, Hindus also believe it is essential to balance karmic debt, learning to clear it and then not accrue more.

What is Karma?

Karma is spiritual accountability for our actions. Karma is not commonly thought of as good or bad fortune but rather taking responsibility for our actions and their results.

The Akashic Record Keepers also tell us that karma is not a punishment—it is a way to facilitate learning for soul growth. As we balance, release, and stop accruing more karma (missed lessons) and come into a place of unconditional love and compassion, we get off the karmic wheel. We can then choose to reincarnate to assist others or to not reincarnate on Earth. There are many other places to travel and visit in all of the multi-dimensional universes.

I find it interesting that Buddhist teachings include reincarnation as an animal. The Akashic Masters tell me that it is rare for a person to go from human to animal, although it occasionally happens, depending on what the soul wants to accomplish or what information they wish to acquire by being an animal.

Why Would I Reincarnate?

Our soul uses different lifetimes to experience other aspects of the physical self that offer different emotions, thoughts, physical limitations and strengths, spiritual explorations, and so much more. The experiences are as limitless as the number of souls living different paths.

We don't always finish all of our lessons before we die. That is why we have many lifetimes, even hundreds, giving us numerous opportunities to complete our work for soul growth. Sometimes, the soul plan is too painful or traumatic for the human to achieve. On a soul level, they might choose to leave that life and wait a while before they can return to try again. We've all created karmic patterns and contracts that are incomplete, and that prompts us to reincarnate, to finish them.

Your Soul Plan May Be a Challenge

Our souls make plans, but it is our free will that chooses whether we can or want to fulfill them.

Of course, we've lived many lifetimes before, learning to be conscious of our acts, words, and deeds. But, as we learn to live a mindful life, when we come to the end of that life, there is a feeling of joy and love, knowing we left the world a better place than when we entered it. Our service to others as well as work, play, and relationships add to a fulfilled life.

In a sense, this does sum up what we, as conscious souls, wish to accomplish. We come to Earth to learn about compassion, gratitude, and forgiveness, and eventually to live in a state of awakening or enlightenment . . . in touch with pure, Divine love.

When the Call Comes

Let's look at the perspective of timing on a soul's plan. When we see our lives from a more expansive viewpoint, we will notice that choices were presented to us to help us learn and grow from challenges, limitations, love, and sorrows. These experiences ready us for the call to service, if that is part of our soul's purpose.

As I mentioned in Chapter 5, the Akashic Record Keepers

came to me and asked me to share this Akashic Record wisdom by making it understandable and teachable to people who were ready for the knowledge.

Part of my soul plan was to assist in bringing the Akashic Record wisdom back to humanity at this time in history. My current soul plan helped my soul to choose when that time would come. At that time, the Akashic Record Keepers would attempt to reach out to me through the intuitive readings I did for my clients. They talked to me and gave me comprehensive information about my clients' soul paths. This went on for over five years, yet I never asked, *Who is giving me this profound and expanded information?*

If they had tried to reach me earlier, without success, it's because I wasn't in alignment yet. Finally, when I was ready to hear the wisdom and allow more profound information to come through me, the perfect clients appeared to be the recipients. The expanded information finally triggered me to ask where that profound wisdom originated.

I became a Certified Prayer Practitioner with the Centers for Spiritual Living, RRCP. That ten years of training and healing work prompted the Record Keepers to ask me to write my second book, *From Questioning to Knowing—73 Prayers to Transform Your Life.* The book includes seventy-three prayers imbued with Akashic healing energy. But over the last thirty years, the most important information I've received from the Akashic Record Keepers has been direct and clear guidance. They are pure, Divine beings of light, without judgment.

Why So Many Lifetimes?

The Akashic Masters tell us that most souls who come to Earth live hundreds of lives here. We often get caught up in learning or not learning, which leads to us returning to learn the same lessons in other lifetimes. This leads to more questions about reincarnation and the number of lives. The Record Keepers say many souls on Earth have been here repeatedly for hundreds, and some thousands, of years. Because of the density of this plane and the challenges life has presented over the past thousands of years, you might have already lived 400 or 700 lives on Earth alone.

We return to break vows, karmic ties, and patterns, and to fulfill contracts. Some of us still have vows affecting our lives that are centuries old, such as vows of poverty, chastity, and obedience. These might be holdovers from our lifetimes as monks, priests, nuns, or as part of other religious sectors. We might be trying to find love, make money, or live an independent and fruitful life, only to be thwarted each time we get close. Those are circumstances we can identify and clear in our soul's Akashic Record. I've enclosed a prayer to help with the release of old vows. Even if you don't think you have them, try this prayer anyway; you never know.

Since we are immortal souls, we've lived in many places, such as other planets or realms, in addition to Earth. Even though this planet is the most demanding of all the planes, with so much to learn, it is a place where we can fully enjoy the physical realm. We revel in the goodness of delicious food; a gorgeous planet with oceans, beaches, mountains, and waterfalls; and so much more glory and magnificence. The beauty here makes our journeys so much more enjoyable.

We love the experience of human touch and intimacy as well as being able to be Creator Beings. We can even create babies and give birth. According to the Akashic Masters, our Earth is unique in all the dimensions and planets where we can live or visit.

Most importantly, as we claim our roles as Creator Beings, we will know and feel it in our hearts so we can embrace and embody it. Our future is mutable; nothing is written in stone. Our life is not predestined. We have choice and free will. We incarnate so we can make conscious choices and decisions that help us learn the truth of our souls and our purposes.

EXERCISE FOR REFLECTION

1. Do you think you've lived more than one lifetime? Why?

2. Have you ever gone somewhere or met someone that felt very familiar to you? Who or what?

3. Have you had a pet that you feel you had lived with in another lifetime?

4. Do you think you might have uncanceled vows affecting your life? What are they?

PRAYER TO RELEASE PAST LIFE VOWS

Mother, Father, Goddess, God, I align to the present in this very moment.

I have experienced blocked energy in my life and in my body.

I now know this is not who I am.

I go into the past, into lifetimes holding vows of poverty.

I now release those vows to the Divine Energy of Source.

I am grateful for all the gifts those lifetimes have given me.

I now claim all my highest good, wisdom, and truth that I can hold.

I walk forward, cleared of past life energy, fears, and blocks as

I embrace my abundant life. I am abundance.

PRAYER FOR MULTI-DIMENSIONAL CLEARING

Mother, Father, Goddess, God, I ask for you to clear
any negative influences from other dimensions and to invite
specific healings and encouragement from another dimension.
I ask my Akashic Beings of Light to assist in the
multi-dimensional clearing of negative input and imprinting.
I ask my future self, who has already achieved this healing and
knows the path, to show me the road filled with grace.
I see the Golden Healing Light of Source come into my body as
I receive wisdom and guidance for my healing journey.
I accept this blessing with gratitude.
So it is. Blessed Be.

In the next chapter, we will discover how emotional pain and trauma may be affecting your ability to create a happy life.

CHAPTER 7

TRAUMA = BLOCKS TO FREEDOM

We write our soul plan before returning to Earth, and this plan covers what we want to experience in the next life. We have many decisions to make, including the contracts we want to start and complete, the karma we want to release, and the lessons and training we will need to achieve our higher soul's purpose. Then, we establish contracts with other souls to ensure we reach the goal of our plan.

We create particular contracts with some people, to cause specific situations. Often, there is some level of emotional trauma included in the soul contract. We might have come to heal abuse in our family line. Before we come to Earth, we make a contract with a soul to work on the abuse. They may choose to be the perpetrator of abuse in our life, leaving us to be the victim in the situation. Or we might be the victim in one life while being the perpetrator in another. In a karmic pattern that lasts over many lifetimes, we may trade roles again and again until we both understand and heal the pattern.

Why would we want to have trauma in our lives, or be the person inflicting the trauma? That is a complicated question with many answers. This is the easiest way to explain why we attract trauma: We want to experience all aspects of trauma because we grow from traumatic experiences. For example, it might be the soul's goal to learn about forgiveness, or we might need to understand the dynamics of compassion after traumatic experiences. The Record Keepers want us to be compassionate and to understand that the perpetrator of trauma is not evil. They might appear bad in this lifetime, but as a soul, they are Divine beings.

In some lifetimes, we succeed in our soul's plan, but in others, we must repeat the challenge and go through the same lessons again until we finally learn.

Each lifetime is a journey in learning about what freedom looks like for us. Unfortunately, trauma is one of our most outstanding teachers because it can happen to us in many ways, on many levels. We can be traumatized on the mental, emotional, spiritual, and physical levels, including through body language and both non-verbal and verbal cues. And we can do the same to others.

Why Would We Do That to Ourselves?

We want to learn and finish past-life lessons relating to trauma and then release the stuck emotions. There may be karmic patterns where we continue to experience life as a perpetrator or a victim. Or we might want to understand how those stuck emotions and karmic patterns influence our lives.

As I previously mentioned, there are many lifetimes when we learned to be conscious of our acts, words, and deeds, and then crossed over into a state of joy and love. We left the world a better place than when we entered it. And for the lifetimes we were not as successful, we will repeat these lessons until we stop harming ourselves and others. We will learn to make a conscious choice to stop, learn, and love.

Remember, we have come to Earth to learn about compassion, gratitude, and forgiveness, so that we can eventually live in a state of awakening or enlightenment and experience pure, Divine love. At times, we must go through the experience of trauma to get to freedom.

Understanding How Our Emotions Help Our Journey

Our highly complex emotions are held deep within us. If we go through lifetime after lifetime ignoring and suppressing our feelings, they will show up at some point, wreaking havoc on our relationships, health, or mental outlook. Illnesses are often the consequence of long-term, suppressed emotions.

Research shows that poorly managed negative emotions are detrimental to your health. For example, negative attitudes and feelings of helplessness and hopelessness can create chronic stress, which upsets the body's hormone balance, depletes the brain chemicals required for happiness, and damages the immune system. Over time, this state can lead to illness and physical pain.

Our inability to give or receive love or to relate deeply with others is another effect of low-vibrational emotions. When we identify our traumas and free that energy through awareness, healing, and forgiveness of ourselves, we can return to a natural state of love. Another benefit of healing is that our creative energy starts to flow, activating the connection to the abundance of all we are to experience in this life.

A soul plan considers what is to be energetically released in suppressed emotions, because we know we won't consciously remember our soul plan when we are born. When I access the Akashic Records for a client, I often see that their biggest block to creating a happy and prosperous life has direct links to childhood and unconscious, past-life traumas.

Judy Had to Start Again

Judy was at a crossroads in her life when she asked me to access her Akashic Records. She'd been studying spiritual teachings with different modalities for more than ten years and decided to start a business as a healer. However, as she began to make plans, her body froze in place because of inflammation. She became petrified at the thought of starting her own business, and her body reacted in kind. Judy wasn't just a little fearful; she felt an irrational fear, verging on terror. She had no idea why her reaction was so visceral or why it affected her body with physical disease.

We got on a phone call to ask, in her Akashic Records, where the terror had originated. The Akashic Masters shared that the terror was a direct emotional trigger from her many lifetimes of persecution. She had been jailed, tortured, and even killed for speaking her truth and sharing her gifts. Judy had spent many lifetimes as a healer and midwife with an expansive toolkit, including herbs, natural remedies, and energy healing. In some of her past lives, during the Holy Inquisition, priests had her tortured and killed.

Her immediate, visceral experience, though unconscious, carried memories of the traumas, pain, and torture. Her body was trying to "save" her by creating inflammation and stopping her forward motion. Those lifetimes had directly sparked fear in her so that she could discover and heal these emotional wounds. However, her soul plan had a higher purpose and needed accomplishing. The soul knew the old traumas needed to be released to allow powerful energy to flow into her work as a healer.

Judy also had childhood trauma triggering her unconscious

memories and accentuating her fear. In her current life, her parents were Christian fundamentalists who believed people would go to Hell as sinners unless they worked hard to become righteous. As a result, Judy spent her childhood praying for forgiveness for her sins, even though she didn't know what her sins were. She feared Hell too much not to pray.

Such a traumatic childhood can trigger old, unconscious memories from past lives. For Judy, it caused the terror that came up when she considered helping people with her gifts of healing energy, prayer, and hands-on healing.

Judy's story is just one of many stories of clients finding the traumatic triggers that limit their happiness and abundance. Yet, in every client's case, traumatic experience was part of their soul plans.

Judy's soul knew the world would desperately need her gifts of healing to humanity to free them. But before she could help the world, she needed to unlock the energy blocking her ability to express herself.

Here's Another Way to View Trauma on the Soul's Plan

Judy had lived other past lives when she planned to use her gifts again, but she was scarred emotionally from multiple lifetimes when she endured pain and death. Those fears blocked her ability to access the well-honed skills needed to create a successful business serving clients. This time, Judy needed to rediscover and relearn how to use her gifts and to overcome whatever or whoever stood in her way of using them.

When she had made her soul plan for this life, she'd decided to be born into a fundamentalist family whose beliefs would trigger her past-life trauma, influencing her current fear of being seen and speaking her truth. She had believed that, by facing some of the challenges at a young age, she would heal them early in life and still have time to bring her gifts out to humanity.

Reclaiming Past Life Gifts and Talents

Judy needed to clear all the past lives filled with the traumas of emotional and physical pain from imprisonment, torture, and death, as well as the emotional pain of growing up in a dysfunctional family. I used a powerful healing tool I received from the Akashic Record Keepers called Akashic Soul Retrieval™. I was able to assist her in reclaiming pieces of her soul that had splintered off because of the emotional trauma. We then could reclaim past-life skills and talents from numerous lifetimes, including lives as a healer, a medicine woman, a shaman, and even a lifetime as an oracle.

Judy felt the energy of the trauma release and move out of her body. After a few follow-up Akashic Healing sessions, she felt her alignment as a qualified healer, so she opened her business and told everyone she knew about her healing work.

Emotional pain from Childhood

Childhood trauma is another main energy block to having the freedom to create the life our soul intends for us. The emotional pain of growing up in a dysfunctional family often gets forgotten and suppressed. It's just too painful to think about or deal with, so we bury it. As adults, we forget about our early life's emotional pain and trauma. If you had a traumatic childhood, you might have locked away the painful memories, assuming they were no longer affecting you. You might have never thought about them or even remembered what happened.

I was working with a client who wanted better relationships with her family of origin, as she carried a lot of anger and upset at her parents. She was happily married with two children and didn't want her anger toward her parents to affect her small children. She was trying to get to the root cause of her anger. I asked her Akashic Record Keepers where it originated and how to clear it. They told us that her anger stemmed from abandonment issues from her current life and six past lives.

When I told her what they had said, she explained that her mother had died when she was only two but that her aunt had stepped in, married her father, and become her mom. My client's anger stemmed from being a two-year-old who had just lost her mother. She had felt sad, scared, and abandoned. Yet no one, including her father, acknowledged her loss. Instead, the newly formed family acted as though nothing had happened or was wrong. They chose not to talk about the death of her birth mother.

The family thought it best not to dwell on her mother's death, believing that, if they just ignored it, she would forget about losing her mom. But she didn't. Her emotions began to surface once she had her own children. Her aunt had felt forced to step into her dead sister's life to raise her daughter. The aunt felt unseen and abandoned because she thought she never had a choice in creating her own life. Both child and aunt were feeling similar experiences, but they didn't communicate with each other, which caused the anger.

Akashic Record Keepers offered clearing of the stuck emotional pain, loss, and abandonment feelings that the two-year-old was still feeling in her thirty-five-year-old body. Even though she didn't consciously dwell on her childhood trauma of losing her mom and having her aunt take her place, she realized she had stuffed all the hurt and loss deep down so as not to feel it. Now she was experiencing the ramifications in her life, and the pain showed up as anger.

The Record Keepers also suggested that she spend two months working on forgiveness for herself and her family. Forgiveness would help her to clear karma throughout time and space. They suggested she keep a gratitude journal. By doing these simple techniques, she could heal her past, including anything that had happened before that moment—both her childhood pain, and past-life trauma.

Even though her healing process may take a few months, she was consciously on the path of releasing and healing the stuck emotional pain from her childhood trauma. She continues to heal by working in her own Akashic Records, as she loved the work so much that she became a student of mine.

I have enclosed the *Prayer of Forgiveness* in Chapter 4, as most people have some aspect of forgiveness work to do. Please add it to your list of daily prayers. You may find it's time to forgive someone or yourself for past occurrences. We often need to forgive ourselves for belittling ourselves for not being smart, pretty, healthy, or wealthy. We can be so hard on ourselves. Please—forgive yourself.

EXERCISE FOR REFLECTION

1. On a scale of one to ten, with ten being the highest, how would you rate your ability to receive compassion and love?

2. Where in your body can you feel repressed anger?

3. Are you ready to release your anger against another or yourself? Name those people and the reason you are angry at them or yourself.

PRAYER TO RELEASE REPRESSED ANGER

Mother, Father, Goddess, God, take my anger, whether from this or another lifetime, from another person or me.

Please transform it through the power of your loving alchemy.

Burn it in the cleansing Fire of the Divine or send it back to wherever it belongs.

Please help me to go beyond the relationships and circumstances that created it so I may know my true purpose and power in this lifetime.

I now release all anger from the depths of my unconscious and stand in the light of clear, pure energy.

With great thanks, I let it go.

So it is. Blessed be.

PRAYER TO RELEASE LOW VIBRATION

Mother, Father, Goddess, God, as I become present in this very moment,

I ask for your assistance clearing any low vibrations held in my body.

I am grateful for the clearing I have received

in my emotional centers, lower chakras, and heart.

I move forward with ease.

So it is. Blessed Be.

PRAYER TO RECEIVE HIGH VIBRATIONAL FREQUENCIES

Mother, Father, Goddess, God, please help me to align from the tips of my toes, straight through my body to the top of my crown chakra.

Please connect me energetically to Creator/Source and help me to receive the highest vibrational frequencies my body can hold right now.

Please assist me in integrating the higher frequencies with ease and grace.

My body accepts this higher vibrational healing,

And is enlivened at a cellular level.

So it is. Blessed Be.

In the next chapter, I will explain how confusion affects our plan.

CHAPTER 8

CONFUSION = MISALIGNMENT

M any clients come to me because they feel unclear or confused about a path they are drawn to. Some are not sure if it's really the right one. Often, fear and other influences from past lives will crop up and leave us in a confused state. It's not clear where the thoughts or feelings are coming from. We are either getting too much or not enough information to move forward. The confusion, which may be unconsciously from past memories, causes paralysis in our thinking, decision-making, and action-taking. We start to overthink our fears, causing paralysis. The logical answer doesn't always make sense regarding soul work because this work is not about logic; it's about the soul's wisdom.

Countless clients have come to me for an Akashic Consultation, many with the big question, "What is my purpose?" or "Have I fulfilled my purpose?" The idea that each person has one purpose is misleading and has been bantered around in spiritual circles for a long time. It's a confusing idea, since few people have had any teaching or understanding about what Soul Purpose really means. Frequently, they feel lost; they have not found their "purpose" and don't know what else it could be.

Their worry about this situation raises these questions:

"What if I make the wrong choice and I go broke?"

"What if I leave my job and then find out that I'm not skilled enough?"

"What if I don't listen to my intuition? And if so, is there karma to pay?"

Our minds are limitless when finding reasons to not follow our dreams and inner guidance. My clients sometimes call their confusion "the abyss" because they feel they will never find their way out of it. They have become overwhelmed, leading to self-doubt and paralysis with no movement forward. Overwhelm is a one-way road leading to lack, confusion, and fear.

Can Confusion and Doubt Cause Misalignment with Your Soul Plan?

This state can cause a misalignment in our soul's yearning to follow its plan. Most people living life are following both unspoken and spoken protocols based on societal norms and the expectations of their parents. Yet, as life goes on, we feel something is not aligned, and this starts showing up in areas of our lives and bodies. Life feels exhausting, and we often end up burnt out and miserable.

We fall into the lower vibration of society's expectations rather than follow the guidance from within. We follow our thoughts and discount our feelings. As time goes on, our spirit starts to rebel. This can show up as physical pain or illness, or an even more extreme wake-up call. Serious illness, accidents, getting fired from a job we're bored with, or leaving a relationship may be ways our soul tries to shake us out of our numbness.

Your soul does not want you to be hurt in following your plan. Instead, it wants you to feel supported on the journey. Your soul knows, without a doubt, that you will find your way out of confusion and misalignment and into untapped potential that is waiting to be discovered and explored. It isn't about leaving relationships, numbing out, or quitting your job to feel better. The journey of your soul has detours and re-routes when needed. It is all part of the process of living life.

Life is a journey. This winding road we follow is part of the plan. It's not a mistake, even though we may judge it so.

Many People Hide Their Boredom and Discontent

We have created hundreds of ways to distract ourselves, including constant shopping or other addictive behaviors such as alcohol, drugs, food, or sex.

I asked the Akashic Record Keepers if these distractions created more karmic patterns. They answered:

> *Once you consciously understand you have gotten lost on the path, you can realign with your soul's plan. This is one of the main reasons people search for ways to access their Akashic Records. They wish to understand where they are, what thinking is aligned with their soul plan and what are some of the steps they can take to move forward. Remember that your soul wants you to succeed and not suffer in any way on the journey to fulfilling your plan.*

Meet Sarah

Sarah is one of my tech clients who knew she would make an impact with her strong ability to communicate information in an understandable and digestible way. However, she was confused about why those around her were not accepting the wisdom she wanted to share. As a result, self-doubt inhibited her ability to move forward confidently.

Although wildly successful as a tech executive, Sarah wanted out, so she could fulfill her soul's yearning to share teachings she had learned along her own path of self-discovery. Unfortunately, although she knew what she wanted to do, she could not find an opening to explore her soul's plan further. At every turn, her talents weren't the right fit. Finally, confused about whether she was following her soul's path, Sarah booked a call with me to receive guidance from her Akashic Masters.

Her first questions were filled with doubt about whether she really was supposed to share the knowledge she had been receiving. The Record Keepers told her she was following her path but needed some adjustments to align more succinctly with her life purpose and soul's plan. They told her about past lives when she was powerful and her words had been important to people.

They explained all that was needed was for her to expand her message so more people could see the value in the individual lessons and wisdom she had to offer. The Record Keepers also explained to her that it is important that she look at her job as a place to incubate her ideas until they are fully formed before she leaves employment. They asked her to consider her current position as a means of income and security. Leaving now could create confusion and stop forward motion, if money became scarce.

As we worked on her doubt and constriction, Sarah felt an immediate release of the energy that had held her in a confused state. Finally, she understood that not being accepted by those around her wasn't because they didn't support her ideas; instead, her message needed tweaking to be more easily understood.

According to the Akashic Record Keepers, Sarah's soul had

set up her job—where she used some of her technical gifts and practiced her communication skills—so she could make a salary that supported her as she moved forward, honing her spiritual talents and teachings.

Your Current Job May Be Exactly What Your Soul Needs

Many lightworkers believe they are not on their soul path if they work at a corporate job. But that is often not the case. You might be working in technical positions, as an engineer, in management, at a bank, or as a lawyer, and that might be the perfect place for your soul to grow and assist humanity. You are there to hold a higher vibration for those around you, to assist in helping the people within the corporations to become more consciously aware.

When people find themselves at a crossroads—whether they are newly divorced or retired, wanting to change jobs, or considering a move to a new city—accessing their Akashic Records can be the perfect path to clarity. As we discussed in Chapter 5, you have more than one purpose, and it's not always connected to a job. Some people find a way to turn their talents into a career or business, but most do not.

Many people never reach the clarity needed to make new choices with direction and purpose. I always find that sad, because the soul has a plan to help us. Look at it as the GPS system we need to access and utilize, rather than spend a minute longer in the space of confusion or uncertainty.

Let's say you share your gifts, but it's not quite what you imagined. Confusion can creep in when something is not what you expected. Expand your sense of self to think of new possibilities that you haven't imagined before. You might be here at this time to assist in healing our planet. Many ancient souls living on Earth today have made soul contracts with Mother Earth, also known as Gaia. Although we usually think of the Earth as a location, she is a sentient being. The Earth is not just a mass of rock, dirt, and water . . . she has consciousness.

Soul Purposes Have Many Paths

Long before they were born, many lightworkers lined up as souls to come to Earth. They wished to assist in healing Gaia, which involves helping to awaken humanity, so they will stop polluting and poisoning our home. This is a profound soul's purpose. However, because it is such an intense and multi-faceted responsibility, many light workers are confused as to how they, as one soul, can help heal Gaia. Soul plans work in millions of different ways.

Let's say you chose an ecology career because you want to be working outdoors. What would your soul plan look like? You might become an environmental consultant, a research scientist, or a park ranger. Other options, and there are many, could be working with communities to build recycling centers. You might start recycling at your children's school or start a business that sells recycled goods as a school fundraiser. Or you may join a group that cleans your local beaches a few times a year.

Most types of soul contracts attached to your purpose can be smaller and less time-consuming; they might become a hobby, or an all-encompassing, full-time career. But even if you were a park ranger or research scientist, you might not realize that it's part of your soul plan; you might think of it as a job that seemed interesting because you like nature and the outdoors.

Some individuals feel drawn to do something they think may be too big, thus becoming overwhelmed. For example, many people feel drawn to being a healer, publishing a book, teaching self-empowerment training and spiritual modalities, or inventing something to assist humanity.

As I work on this book, the Record Keepers remind me of a

therapist-client who wanted to become a healer. However, she felt her profession did not align with her soul's purpose.

The message from her Akashic Record Keepers reminded her:

You are already a healer. In time you will add more energy modalities, but your work reaches many people and heals them for now. Feel the truth and healing of the work you are doing. Feel the energetic connection to your client's soul as you help them heal the problems they faced when they first came to you. You can study more about what interests you in the healing arts, and you will know when you are ready.

The Akashic Masters remind us:

You are infinite and wise. If a path speaks to your Heart, it is part of your purpose, no matter how unusual or impossible it may seem to you.

Remember, when you are confused, you may make rash decisions not aligned with your higher purpose. Do not just jump into the first thing that catches your eye. Whether a new job, a class, or a trip to a sacred site, if you are misaligned, that new step falls short, leaving you with more confusion and frustration. You may get distracted with anger or feel like a failure.

You have misinterpreted a situation while in "Searching Mode." You are looking so hard that you forgot to breathe and allow your soul's plan to unfold. The stress and anxiety that comes when a new step doesn't work out can contribute to the feeling of being unworthy. You may think, "I tried and failed; it must not be meant to be." But do not give up, as you are a soul learning how to align with your soul's purpose and plan for it. You are One with the Divine energy of Source and a gift to humanity.

Why Are We Challenged?

Misalignment can show up in many ways; maybe you have challenges with the people at your new job or you realize that you don't quite resonate with a course you started. When misalignment is extreme, we can become ill or miss every appointment we have lined up. These can be seen as a multitude of signals letting us know we are not aligned.

We might stumble if we take a leap without checking to find out how it feels in our hearts. A powerful practice to start is to ask your inner wisdom and spirit if a step is in alignment with your soul and heart's desire. There is nothing wrong with a stumble, because it can serve as a growth point with lessons learned and wisdom gained. You wish to learn. Or a misstep might be part of a karmic pattern you came to understand and release. Those experiences may be part of your soul's plan.

We can learn to make fewer mistakes, but we should not fear errors because they are learning experiences. Learn to listen to your heart's guidance, but don't worry too much about making mistakes. All challenges can be viewed as positive when they are part of your soul growth.

───────────── **EXERCISE FOR REFLECTION** ─────────────

1. What is a challenge you have recently been going through?

2. When did you start to notice it?

3. What are some of your common distractions? How are they impeding your success?

PRAYER TO REALIZE WHAT I DON'T KNOW

Mother, Father, Goddess, God, as my Heart expands to open a new door, please help me also expand my mind to know the questions I've never thought of before.

Help me realize what is essential and valuable for me now.

So it is. Blessed Be.

PRAYER FOR ALIGNMENT

Mother, Father, Goddess, God, please show me what it feels like to be the Highest, Brightest, most Expansive, and Aligned Self that I can be today.

Please open my Heart to know the truth of my Divinity and allow me to receive all the good within and without.

Please guide me on my next steps to being

Abundant in all ways, with ease and Grace.

So it is. Blessed Be.

Now that you have learned how doubt and confusion create misalignment, it's time to dive into reclaiming past talents.

CHAPTER 9

IDEAS
= SOUL'S PLAN

Each time your soul decides to return to Earth, you write a plan based on various lifetimes that still have karma and contracts you'd like to complete. You also gather many talents and training from previous lifetimes and a critical skill set you have already fine-tuned for this life. Your quest is to rediscover your talents to fulfill your multiple purposes.

I find our life's purposes are much more complex than knowing about our talents and gifts, but claiming those gifts is part of a path to self-discovery and fulfillment. Many detours can cause us to take the long road instead of the short one, which is part of the fun and challenge of coming to Earth to grow as a soul.

Your soul purpose is also about completing karmic patterns that keep you from connecting to your passions. As we realize that our challenges are not punishment but come from our soul's desire to develop, we can reframe them so they become more manageable. We start to move through blocked energy quickly as we access the creative process that makes dreams a reality.

The purpose of a plan is to assist in awakening a memory that will ignite our curiosity to discover who we are as a Divine soul. That is why we can have dreams so much bigger than we believe we could accomplish. The soul plan pushes us toward a more fantastic version of ourselves by giving us the passion for following our dreams.

Communicating with the Beings of Light of Your Akashic Records

My work with clients in Akashic Records helps to give them insight and shortcuts in knowing with certainty that this is the direction to take. By receiving soul guidance with the Akashic Masters' information, which was not formerly available, you can make an educated choice. Your soul knows the truth.

One challenge most people have in this physical world is to discover what is unconscious and make it conscious. Sometimes you might have had an inkling that you were going in the right direction, or you just knew you were to follow a particular path. Your Record Keepers open the door to wisdom you didn't know you had. It is up to you to follow the path, challenges and all.

Unrelenting Ideas Are from Your Soul's Plan

Steven is a client who came to me because he kept getting an idea for a product that could help improve people's lives. It was utterly new and a bit outside the box, as nothing like it had been invented yet. He was happy with his career and had been working in a fulfilling job as a successful engineer more than over ten years, but this nagging idea kept coming to him, month after month. Eventually, he knew he needed information from his higher consciousness, his soul, to find out what he was supposed to do.

This idea was driving him, yet his fears made him question moving forward.

Steven knew he had never invented anything before, which caused him to question his qualifications to produce such a product. However, when we were working in his Akashic Records, he discovered three past lives when he had been a creative designer or inventor. These lifetimes varied and were hundreds and even thousands of years ago. In one of his lives, we were shown that he had been an inventor of the early water wheel in 40 B.C., and that knowledge had helped him in other lifetimes. In another life, he had tried to invent a better mechanical clock; in the third, in the 1800s, he was part of a team of engineers working on the telegraph. This information was integral to Steven's validation to move forward with his ideas for a new invention.

Your Akashic Record is a Vast Library

Imagine your own Library of Congress times thousands. That's how extensive your Akashic Library is. The information is there for you to access when you're looking for clarity, you need to clear old karmic patterns, you want to discover the root of your limiting patterns, and you know it's time to reclaim your ancient training, talents, and knowledge. Your soul plan wants you to succeed. It's up to you to determine how you want to access the information and how long you would like to be in a state of confusion about what your next steps will be.

The Record Keepers share that some souls still carry trauma from the Inquisition, the horror of which has been well-documented. For 500 years, many women and some men with healing arts, talents, and gifts were accused of being witches. Some were hanged, if they were lucky, and others met worse fates. Their physical pain and emotional trauma left a lasting scar on their souls. That scar shows up as fear or emotional pain in other lifetimes. It might make you believe that it's not safe to be seen, leading you to live a sheltered life instead of following your soul's plan to become all that you can.

Because you are an ancient soul, you most likely have layered your past-life traumas with emotional or physical challenges in this life. We know, as old souls, that we often need trials or traumas to trigger us to realize and remember more about who we are as infinite souls. We want to heal the emotional pain and trauma because behind that pain is often a gift. It might be a talent or a new alignment you've wanted so you could move forward to create your own business. Or it might be the gift of finally completing a karmic pattern that has escaped you for more than fifteen lifetimes.

We May Feel Disassociated from Life Because of Trauma

I often see another, more subtle challenge in the Akashic Records. It is one of the reasons that we don't feel complete or capable of stepping into the aspect of our soul plan which our soul wishes to express. Whether becoming an inventor, authoring a book, or starting a business, we feel afraid to follow our vision.

When we endure a significant physical and emotional trauma, the soul might splinter or create a fragment that stays behind. We lose a piece of our soul, which separates from us so we can survive the experience by escaping the full impact of the pain. *Dissociation* is one of the more common symptoms of trauma, a symptom that includes not feeling fully in one's body and not fully engaging in life. Other symptoms may include:

- Depression
- Suicidal tendencies
- Post-traumatic stress syndrome

- Immune deficiency problems
- Grief that does not heal
- Addictions

In the past, Soul Retrieval was used. This process, typically guided by an experienced shaman, involved bringing the lost bit of soul back. First, the shaman reached an altered state of consciousness to go into the unseen realms of Spirit to find the soul fragment. Then they addressed whatever caused the soul to split off, and then brought the fragment back into this plane to rejoin with the larger soul.

Some modern hypnotherapists specialize in a form of soul retrieval. The client is hypnotized and journeys back in time to relive the trauma and heal the pain, thereby reclaiming the soul splinter.

With your permission, the Akashic Masters will assist in an Akashic Healing Session to clear old fears and traumas. They can also retrieve lost soul fragments and splinters from this life or another lifetime. When we reclaim the soul fragments, if that is part of the intention, we also reclaim our unique talents.

Releasing the entangled blockages from past lives can feel like a surge of energy. This process is unconditional love in action. It is my honor to partner with the Akashic Masters to heal those seeking to reclaim their wisdom, gifts, soul fragments, and empowerment tools from past lives.

This book is a physical manifestation of how the Record Keepers and I are partners to facilitate identifying and reclaiming your gifts, wisdom, and tools.

EXERCISE FOR REFLECTION

1. What ideas have been coming to you in your dreams or intuition?

2. Do some of these dreams feel too big for you to accomplish?

3. What or who is stopping you from moving forward?

PRAYER TO RELEASE ILLUSION

Mother, Father, Goddess, God, please open my heart and connect me to multi-dimensional universes.

Help me to remember that this life is only one in the myriad of lives on Earth and elsewhere.

I am an Infinite Soul, and I release the illusion that I am just a small, fearful human.

I step into the grand image of who and what I truly am.

So it is. Blessed Be.

PRAYER OF SELF-TRUST

Mother, Father, Goddess, God, I awaken to the memory of the ancient soul I am.

I know I can trust myself and my inner guidance with this memory.

I am a Divine soul with a human experience that is good.

So it is. Blessed Be.

PRAYER FOR STRENGTH

Mother, Father, Goddess, God, at this moment, I connect with you as I remember the strength of who I am.

Please assist me in continuing on my soul path,

To do what my soul has come to do, even if I am not yet conscious of that path.

I give great thanks for the strength that fills my body now.

I am blessed and filled with gratitude.

In the next chapter, we look at creating greater abundance in our lives.

CHAPTER 10

COLLECTIVE GIFTS = ABUNDANCE

The soul comes to flourish in this lifetime. No matter how complex and challenging your soul's plan is, your soul knows you can handle it. You are infinite and eternal. That is not to mitigate the fact that most of humanity lives in sub-human conditions with tremendous physical and emotional pain and trauma. The Akashic Masters have shared that we choose to come to Earth to overcome!

You are truly ancient, with thousands and thousands of lives, not only here on Earth but in many other planes and dimensions. This simply means we have had many opportunities to learn and hone our talents and gifts and to experience many different levels of wealth.

You may be challenged to discover your purpose or create an abundant life in this lifetime. Alternatively, you might be using your gifts and skills, enjoying the wealth of money and friends, but lacking a good health. Abundance is still a challenge if you have wealth, but not in the areas most people expect. We are trained to think abundance is about money.

Part of everyone's sole purpose is to be abundant in *all* ways, including health, vitality, love, joy, peace, and wealth. When you overcome an obstacle, you have received a great gift of learning, perception, and growth that can increase your sense of abundance. You can then share the wisdom you've gained with people in your life. One of our most essential soul purposes is to share our knowledge.

You may choose to teach, write, or speak about your own journey in a more public way. Or you might share it with your children, friends, and family members individually. We also share our learned wisdom with other souls around the universe and in other worlds.

Your soul wants to let go of karmic patterns so you can embrace true abundance by reclaiming the collective gifts it has accumulated over the many lifetimes you've already lived. This is why each soul's plan has various options, just in case the cues and intuitive signals to act are missed.

Why Do We Limit Ourselves?

As ancient souls, we understand that we need not limit ourselves, as the universe's abundance is infinite, just like you. The abundance or lack that we experience in our lives is often a matter of unconscious choices and inaction. If a door opens and we don't walk through it, it will likely close. Procrastination and indecision are two of the big blocks to greater abundance, though there are many other layers.

Some of the levels and layers of information that come up when I do Akashic Healing sessions for clients are:

Childhood beliefs that are often unconscious. Some of these come from the way parents speak to their children: "We can't afford that," "That's a waste of money," and "You don't deserve that!"

Childhood trauma, abuse, and emotional pain that led us to feel unworthy. This might show up as self-sabotage and procrastination.

Following another's path: Feeling that we need to choose a specific career, even if it's not really what we want. Having poor boundaries or allowing someone else's desires to make our choices.

Ancestral patterns that you were born with or born into. Stories about struggle and lack include such messages as, "You must work very hard, just to survive." That might look like being underpaid and overworked. Getting passed over for a promotion again and again often is connected to ancestral patterns as well as patterns of low self-worth.

Past lives of poverty and early death, which affect our ability to see ourselves as abundant in this life.

Past-life vows of poverty or vows of unworthiness. We might have vowed "never to be wealthy" because we've been killed for our wealth in a past incarnation. This can block our ability to receive abundance of all kinds in this life.

Soul contracts: We have a variety of soul contracts and group soul contracts that may involve a lack of abundance in some way. Some of these contracts might be with people in this life, and some may be past-life contracts stuck outside of time and space.

Defining Abundance

One of the biggest mistakes we make around money is believing in our limited definition of abundance, including what abundance meant to us in past lifetimes. Abundance isn't always about dollars and cents or material possessions; we often incarnate to experience a profusion of health, love, or creativity.

Our planet offers abundant opportunities to learn, experience, and share our gifts and to reap financial benefits from using them. When we're feeling a lack of any kind, I think nature serves as a perfect example of pure abundance. All you have to do is go into nature to experience its beauty and wonder. Notice the thousands of leaves on the trees and the millions of blades of grass on a lawn. They are countless in their abundance. The wide variety of birds and flowers, with a multitude of colors and designs, offer a lens to view plenty from the soul's definition of abundance and how it fills our lives.

When desiring to build your dreams and garner your well-tooled talents from past lives, you must trust your soul. Its plan was created for this lifetime, to assist you in feeling whole, which equates to abundance. That is true even if you struggle to make a living, forgive wrongdoing, or find a relationship that will support and contribute to your life.

Unfortunately, many people reach a time in their lives when they're ready to receive their abundance, but they feel stuck. Often, the root cause is that they aren't trusting themselves enough to step into the musings they have been receiving from their souls.

Take a moment to acknowledge that you are an ancient soul with numerous past lives filled with collective gifts and experiences, and that you are whole and abundant! How does that feel?

It's easier to know that not everything you think or feel about your current situation is accurate; it might not be necessary for the soul's plan. So often, we define our experiences based on the past. That is why letting go of the old, blocked energy makes it easier to have a larger perspective. Many of our thoughts and feelings are somehow linked to our past, either past lifetimes or the earlier years of this life. Accessing the Akashic Records offers clarity and an expansive understanding of the path you have been on. Your thinking changes so you can realign to your purpose.

Aligning to Your Soul's Purpose

When you align with your soul's purpose, your life flows with information and opportunities not seen before. It may be that they were there but you didn't have the awareness to notice. I compare it to walking into a room you've walked into many times and seeing a painting you'd never noticed before. You think it is new, but it had always been there. Your awareness expanded to take notice of what had been present all along.

That is what happens when you align with your soul's plan. You start to discover and engage your collective talents and gifts. You might not yet have clarity about the path you are to take, but suddenly you can clearly see the next steps. Both you and your purpose are unique. The way your purpose expresses itself will be unlike any other person's.

Our reason for being here is in the plan of our soul. At first, your plan might seem to be in a foreign language you don't understand—but with persistence and pursuing a spiritual practice, understanding your plan gets easier. Doing so will align you with your higher wisdom so that you can discover and learn to trust and enjoy your talents and gifts.

Making Money and Your Soul's Path

Your soul plan is filled with opportunities to grow, learn, and serve by expressing your soul gifts. Money is a means of exchange invented by humans. If having or not having money helps you identify and change old patterns and vows, money might be a central figure in your life.

The Akashic Masters share with my clients:

Financial issues are stumbling blocks that separate you from knowing without a doubt that you already are but do not consciously know your capacity for greatness.

The most significant factor is to embrace what are

considered flaws and assets. Face the fears to regain your knowledge of who you are as a creator. Most things humans fear should not be feared at all. Your soul knew you would succeed, if not this one, in another lifetime. It is your failure you fear in not fulfilling your soul's plan. All other fears fall short of the one we just mentioned.

Fear is Simply a Misunderstanding

Fear is a tool to separate us from the collective gifts and abundance needed to fulfill our purpose. I like to see fear as a misunderstanding or a limited definition of an experience because, as mentioned earlier, fear is often based on past experiences in this lifetime and others. It's time to redefine those experiences by consciously letting go and observing how you feel without fear anchoring you in place.

Start with baby steps in letting go of the fears blocking you from making more money or having a dream job or business. Fears are typically layered. Start with the most obvious and work your way through the layers. If you are like my clients, you might want help to clear the blocked energy so you can move on much more quickly. That is the blessing of having your own Akashic Records and Record Keepers to streamline the process.

Many of my clients describe feeling clear and supported in taking their next steps after I work with their Akashic Masters to release old blocks. For example, you may find yourself looking for a new job because you've decided your old job doesn't pay well. In addition, you may realize you've eliminated the fear of starving if you don't have a paycheck. This is a common fear that may come from other lifetimes where you did starve to death because there was a famine or no work for anyone. If we continue to hold true to the concept of soul abundance, we can bring it deeper within and reach the personal level where layers of fears hide.

Money is Misunderstood

You may have heard the expression, "Money is the root of all evil." That's incorrect; the actual saying is, "The *love* of money is the root of all evil." We're raised to think that wanting to have money is somehow wrong, and the media confirms this.

In film and stories, rich people are often portrayed as selfish and/or cruel —think of Scrooge in *A Christmas Carol.* Those with meager means are typically shown as saintly and loving, such as Bob Cratchit in the same movie. News reports about Mother Teresa, who was well-known for all the charity work she did, label her as the epitome of generosity and kindness because of her poverty.

Because we grew up with so many negative definitions of money and plenty, it's no wonder we are limited in understanding the meaning of our experiences with abundance. We might feel confused about how abundance will affect us, or we might feel we don't deserve it.

At this point in history, we have had two years to reevaluate how we want to live and make money. We are seeing the end of the Covid pandemic and resuming in-person life experiences again, instead of all-virtual interactions. Many of us have started reimagining our lives in a significant way. We might have lost or resigned from our jobs or considered relocating. As a result, many of us are feeling renewed anxiety about work and income.

When we take the worry out of our choices and instead trust our new options, we can further understand our higher purpose for being here at this time. How do these choices and changes affect your abundance?

How We Create Money Karma

The Akashic Masters explain karma differently than you may have heard. They do not see karma as punishment but instead as an incomplete lesson our souls wish to understand, which may appear as a life challenge. Karmic lessons can show up in our engrained patterns around money, relationships, and understanding of the world around us. They affect how we experience life. Unfortunately, when we are stuck in a karmic pattern, we are often oblivious to how it's affecting us and our finances.

We can create money karma in many different ways. You may have had a past life in which you stole money from your employer or a business partner. In your current lifetime, you get fired from a job because of suspicion around your integrity. It feels unfair to you, but this is a karmic lesson showing up to be revisited. Or maybe the lesson is presented when a business partner steals your ideas and opens a new business. Again, this is helping to move you to a place of greater awareness, compassion, and forgiveness.

I'd like for you to change how you relate to karma. Think of it as blocked energy keeping you stuck until you consciously address it by freeing your feelings, your thoughts, or yourself. Pay attention to where you are stuck or the repeating patterns that limit you most, especially with your money. Money karma itself is not good or bad; it is just the energy of imbalance. But this energy can derail you from being successful in your financial endeavors.

Our relationship with money is a leading player in our lives, affecting how we make many choices. If, in this life, we don't come to understand the many relationships we have with value (money) that our soul wishes to learn, we will give ourselves another chance in another lifetime. Coming back provides a new opportunity to fulfill our soul learning, which is why most of us have lived hundreds of human lifetimes.

Collective Unconscious Beliefs

As mentioned, society's thoughts about money also have a powerful effect on us. Ideas about money and prosperity may come from your parents, grandparents, teachers, or religious leaders. Maybe a neighbor or your best friend's parents influenced your views about money.

You might remember your parents saying, *"We can't afford that new bicycle! Do you think money grows on trees?"* Even if they didn't say it, they might have felt it, transferring their thoughts and beliefs to you energetically through facial expressions and body language. We carry around unconscious and nonverbal ideas and opinions about money. In many families and cultures worldwide, money is a taboo subject. These thoughts and beliefs become engrained and unconscious patterns, leading us to limit how we relate to money and its value in our lives. As children, things we can't discuss are usually considered "bad." Far too often, these behaviors are never examined or questioned.

I'd like you to expand your idea of abundance. Understand that your level of wealth isn't about your worth or whether you can reclaim the gifts you wielded in past lives. In your current life, whether you feel abundant or not, step back for a moment to reassess where you are right now. What are some of the dreams and ideas you've put away?

Below are some common beliefs passed down through families and cultures. You might keep yourself from abundance if you believe:

- I don't want to have money because rich people have problems.

- Money is bad.

- Money causes unhappiness.

- People marry you for your money, not because they love you.

- Rich kids party too much and get in trouble.

- Rich people get divorced a lot.

- You have to work really hard to make money.

- You have to be very intelligent to make money; I'm not that smart.

- You have to be born rich to have a lot of money.

- If you have a lot of money, you must have acquired it illegally, so you must be a gangster or crook.

EXERCISE FOR REFLECTION

1. List some of your beliefs about having or not having money.

2. How have they affected your financial choices?

3. Which beliefs on your list are you ready to let go of?

To experience your Divine abundance, you must clear out these negative beliefs. This Akashic healing prayer can help:

PRAYER FOR FINANCIAL ABUNDANCE

Mother, Father, Goddess, God, I am open to the flow of abundance.

Please take me back, outside of time and space,

to the origin of any lack or poverty consciousness I hold.

I release the collective beliefs that affect me consciously and unconsciously.

I liberate any views from my family and ancestral lineage

and return them to their originator with love.

I now create a new space to make new choices in my life and body.

I am free to follow my Soul Path.

As I step into the flow of abundance, new ideas, situations, and opportunities enhance my life with ease.

I accept these blessings for all of humanity.

I am filled with gratitude.

So it is. Blessed be.

PRAYER TO RELEASE JEALOUSY AND COMPETITION

Mother, Father, Goddess, God, please help me to know that I am enough.

There is nothing in the universe that I am not.

I release old beliefs that it is possible to be better or worse.

I know we are all Divine souls on unique journeys with extraordinary gifts.

I give thanks for the gift that I am to the world.

So it is. Blessed Be.

In the next chapter, we look at how we create our various life purposes.

CHAPTER 11

SOUL PLAN = PURPOSE

I often hear people lament, "I just wish I knew what my purpose was." I'm fascinated by the erroneous idea that each of us has a single purpose, and that we're destined to be miserable and deficient until we find it. So many books, blogs, and articles claim to have the formula that enables you to discover your one true purpose. Hogwash!

Can You Have More Than One Purpose?

What exactly is a purpose? Many people think of it as a Divine job description—accountant, doctor, engineer, lawyer, entrepreneur, artist—when it is more important to use the gifts and talents you've accumulated from numerous lifetimes. Specific paths you've chosen in other lives might be a piece of what you're here to do this time, but they don't necessarily equate to one purpose or path.

What I've discovered, on my own journey and supporting clients on theirs, is that most of us have more than one life purpose; often we have three to five purposes. For me, my three have shown themselves in my roles as Communicator, Healer, and Mother. That's not very specific as a job description. We actually plan it that way, because our soul came to use its free will, so we can make many choices and experience the outcome of each.

In hindsight, the discovery of my first life purpose, as a communicator, was no surprise. I loved writing stories in high school and entered college with a journalism major. I then spent years in advertising and cultivated quite a successful career in the corporate world in my twenties and early thirties. These talents and skills—both retained from past lives and acquired in this one— translated easily. I believe that is my over-arching soul purpose. Communicator, for me, has meant everything from advertising executive to author, speaker, Akashic teacher, and consultant. Those positions all fall under this umbrella.

I've known for thirty years that part of my purpose is to share the wisdom of the Akashic Records with humanity and to help people remember the truth of who they are. Over these last thirty years, I've received information about "why" and "how" to bring the Akashic Records to the world. It continues to come in, going deeper with time and capacity. We rarely see or understand all of our path in one moment. The Record Keepers continually remind me that, *Life is a journey, not a destination.*

All aspects of this piece of my purpose require me to be a skilled and thoughtful communicator. I didn't start out that way. I felt great doubt and fear when the Record Keepers first suggested that I become an author to bring this information out to the world. I've worked for years on overcoming shyness and doubt, to speak on thousands of radio shows, podcast, summits, and stages. Communicating the wisdom from the Akashic Records to clients and students daily has been a blessing for me. It has also been tremendously intense work.

In retrospect, now that I've worked in the Akashic Records for three decades, my soul purpose as a healer makes more sense. When I first realized this role as a calling, in my teenage years, it seemed an impossible task. I knew I had lived many lives as a healer of one sort or another: shaman, wise woman, alchemist, oracle, priestess, and Essene. It's clear to me now that, in this lifetime, I came to use this skill to help heal trauma and emotional pain, through the Akashic Records. That is why my soul chose the trauma of loss and abandonment. We often experience pain and trauma so we can learn, grow, and then teach what we've learned.

Healing is essential for human evolution. Without the healing process, you cannot remember the truth of who you are. When I started the Akashic Knowing School of Wisdom, the Record Keepers said to me, *We want you to teach people to read their Soul Records and have the tools to heal themselves of the pain, trauma, and old soul contracts that no longer serve them.* Because this was their mandate, I've added healing tools to my Akashic Record Courses.

The third purpose for me was to be a mother. Some write contracts to be the "Mother of All." That usually equates to a life without our own children but mothering many children in various roles, including mothering other adults. This is often connected to a Divine Mother soul contract.

Realizing that part of my overall purpose included being a mother was a bit curious to me, as I never had any great drive or interest in having kids. When my husband and I decided to have a child, we went from zero to four in less than two years! Through my work in the Akashic Records, I learned I had four soul contracts to be a mother. Three are my natural children—our son and his twin sisters—and one is my nephew, whom I consider to be my son. Remember, you don't need to give birth to a child to fulfill your soul purpose as a mother.

How You Can Find Your Life Purposes

You may already be living in a way that is aligned with your life purposes, but you don't recognize it yet. Many of us wait for that bolt of lightning to show us. We prop our eyes open so we don't miss the special message that reveals this mysterious secret. But that's not the way it happens.

There are three settings in which we live our purposes: work, family, and relationships. If you can't imagine that your current job is already a part of your purpose, I encourage you to examine your work from a different perspective.

A client once came to me asking about his soul purpose, part of which he believed was to share love and wisdom with the people in his life. He couldn't fathom how his job in I.T. was related. When we dug deeper, it became clear that his ability to lead his team with compassion and wisdom fulfilled part of his life purpose. His gift of leadership was being used in a way he hadn't recognized.

What you do for a living is nowhere near as important as how you operate in any given situation. The question is, are you being the highest and best person that you can be today? This includes your relationships as well. You'll know that you are acting in a way aligned with your Life Purpose when you experience peace and contentment inside.

Some people want to make the concept of living their soul's purpose complex and hard to find, but the path is there if you look. Using the gifts that come to you naturally and easily is the foundation of your Life Purpose; to uncover and share them is an ongoing journey.

Because you have more than one purpose, you might find that you are fulfilling one or more at any given time. It's a path that expands and grows as you do. The Akashic Masters are always here to support your discovery, and the prayers they share with me are also valuable.

Moving Forward with Purpose

Throughout the chapters of this book, I've shared with you many different facets of a soul's plan and how you can best decipher its direction. Now that you have enough information to get started, let's dive into consciously moving toward your soul's purpose.

Align to Your Purpose

It's important to be aligned with anything you want to manifest. There is a harmonious flow to our experiences when we are aligned to our souls' plan, doing the work in fulfilling our contracts and sharing our talents. We handle serendipitous situations and opportunities with ease. And often, the opposite is true when we aren't aligned. We get detoured, which leads to struggles and various types of challenges.

I want you to know that just because you've been detoured on your path doesn't mean you won't complete your soul's purposes. Sometimes, a detour becomes a great teacher, as we recognize an old karmic pattern. For example, you may realize you have a habit of distracting yourself when you are close to completing something inspiring, something that you know in your heart is right for you. You've discovered a self-sabotaging pattern. You might get so angry that you finally say: Enough! The result is that you healed your pattern and know that it will not distract you again.

The soul's purpose then becomes more prominent than the distraction. It's an alignment so strong that nothing will get in your way of accomplishing your desire. It is as though you have tunnel vision, and renewed focus is the result.

I know that many of you reading this book have challenges in your life. You are still showing up to have a positive impact, so please show yourself some gratitude. At this time, you might not have clarity on how to define your purpose, or which steps to take next. You can still be proud of the fact that no matter what your challenge may be, it hasn't stopped you from moving forward to look for answers so that you can step into your own, unique soul plan and heal yourself and the world.

Each of us is a unique and Divine soul who has come with many great soul purposes. Yours might be to heal your family trauma and clear old karmic patterns. You may be here to share hope on a difficult path you have conquered. When you know you can help others who are still struggling to find clarity on their path, you have gained the wisdom from your own healing and are now the teacher. You won't know for sure until you start your journey.

Accomplishing great work in the world isn't limited to becoming a famous person or well-known spiritual teacher or healer. Not everyone is here to heal large numbers of people. Some soul plans include healing our family's ancestral line. We can have a talent and purpose to Be the Light or to heal other souls we encounter at a restaurant, on a bus, or in a group of people.

Many people have soul contracts to assist in healing throughout the world; we are the Vessels of Light. Our most important and valuable purpose in life is to be a light-filled vessel and to allow ourselves to do the work we contracted to do. We can accomplish great deeds wherever we choose to be. The more light and grace we can hold, the more light and grace our souls have to offer those souls around us.

If that is your path, fulfilling your soul's purpose can be done quietly in your community, for yourself, and for your family. You might be creating a bridge of light to Gaia, our Mother Earth, which we spoke about earlier. You might be here to save endangered animals or bring new technology to the planet. A lifetime becomes truly great when you live the vision that you have planned out for yourself. But you must begin by aligning with it.

How Do Your Soul Purposes Show Up in Your Life?

Here are a few examples: If your soul purpose is to be a communicator, you may be of service by writing an informational blog and a book. You might speak to groups in your area, sharing the wisdom and gifts your soul came to share. If your book becomes a bestseller, you may share your unique message and knowledge with a larger audience through radio shows. You are clearly fulfilling your soul purpose by being of service to listeners, as well as creating a following, which brings you financial abundance.

Or you may choose to share your gift of communication as a sixth-grade teacher. You express your passion for communication by teaching students to love reading and writing. As a result, you are raising more great speakers and authors for the world.

Let's imagine that one of your soul's purposes is to start a business in partnership with someone you have been best friends with since childhood. Everything goes well until you realize your partner had been stealing from the company without your knowledge. Then, of course, you'll have to deal with feelings of anger and betrayal. But learning to deal with those feelings might be one of your soul's purposes, too.

In soul work, there are always more levels to consider, such as past-life relationships. You may realize through your Akashic Records that your soul has karmic money lessons to complete. In a past life, *you* were the partner who ran off with all the goods, leaving your friend penniless. His betrayal now feels unfair to you initially, but when you and your business partner work through past-life issues and to heal the present life, you start to see a bigger picture. You are both able to work on forgiving each other. You may or may not continue your business together, but either way, you have been transformed through your shared work.

Not all soul purposes start off with success. Sometimes, in order to succeed, you must overcome some karma you would only face as a business owner, in your chosen profession, or in a relationship. For example, working puts you out into the world, which triggers fears of being seen. People with karmic ties to you can find you if you are seen. You will then have a choice to work through the old karmic pattern or continue to hold onto it.

It's most important to remember that your soul wants you to succeed in the plan it has created. Therefore, you will encounter other souls here to support you in your success.

EXERCISE FOR REFLECTION

1. What questions would you ask your Akashic Record Keepers?

2. Which area of your life would you like help with?

3. How do you feel about discovering and following your soul's plan?

PRAYER OF CREATING HEAVEN ON EARTH

As I integrate the power of the soul with the power of the body,

I manifest with ease and grace.

I am a Creator Being with a purpose.

I am now creating Heaven on Earth.

I am blessed and filled with gratitude.

So it is. Blessed be.

PRAYER TO BE A MAGNET FOR GOOD

Mother, Father, Goddess, God, I am a magnet for good.

My magnet energy field is clear and strong as I draw to me the good that is in alignment with my highest path.

I am a powerful magnet for good.

With gratitude.

So it is. Blessed Be.

PRAYER TO KNOW WHAT YOU NEED TO MOVE FORWARD

Mother, Father, Goddess, God, I stand in your grace, clear and strong, humble and full of love.

Please assist me in finding, seeing, and taking the next step on my Soul Path.

I ask for guidance in baby steps and giant steps, too.

I live in self-trust, self-worth, and faith.

I have what I need to do my soul work.

So it is. Blessed Be.

Now let's look at where we are going.

CHAPTER 12

WHERE ARE WE HEADED?

I see so many people becoming conscious of the fact that there is more to life than just the basics. Society has taught us to find a good job, buy a new car, get married, have a family, and own a house. All of this, along with some hobbies and vacations, tends to sum up our lives.

But right now, many people are starting to wake up to the fact that life is much more than a checklist. And when they do, often clients come to me with a variety of emotions, challenges, and odd symptoms. Some are quite aware of this shift in their energy, but many are confused about what is happening to them. Their experiences range from feeling lonely or exhausted to experiencing wonderful synchronicities. All of this can be part of the process of awakening.

Why are People Having a Spiritual Awakening Now?

While there are various reasons that people are waking up now (some of which we've talked about in this book), one of the major reasons is that there is more high vibrational light coming to Earth than ever before. This is part of the Age of Aquarius alignment, a new energetic alignment that supports us to awaken. The vibration of the planet is also escalating, which intensifies our personal experiences and is not always comfortable.

What are the Signs of Awakening?

There are numerous reasons that people are awakening, but the experience is not always easy or fast. One of the common signs is a shift in your perception of the world around you and the work you do. Many people begin to feel detached and alone at this point. Sometimes our friends drift away. We find we no longer have anything in common, and so we stop talking to them. Sometimes we realize that a close friend is negative and draining. We never noticed it before, but now it's hard to be around them.

If we start losing friends, we might blame ourselves and feel that we are doing something wrong. The truth is, we don't resonate with their energy any longer. You might suddenly realize that your friend is always complaining but never willing to make a change. You realize you cannot save them, and the highest choice you can make is to let that relationship go for now.

We may experience a breakup or divorce because we can no longer tolerate anger or abuse from a partner. Sometimes that experience of trauma triggers our awakening, as well. When your dreams and desires are changing, your friends or family may be critical of or uncomfortable with that change.

In fact, drastic shifts of all kinds can trigger our ability to see the world in an expanded way. A severe accident or other big change in our life, such as losing a job or moving, may trigger an awakening.

Sometimes it's meeting someone new or listening to a podcast with new ideas you've never heard before, or even watching a TV show about something unusual to you. Or you might realize that you have a strong calling to start meditating or being of service in some way.

People who are awakening might experience a variety of other symptoms, such as a heightened sensitivity to other people's energy. You may experience vivid dreams or strong intuitive downloads that you've never had before. You might feel sensations in your body or realize you are feeling other people's emotions. Perhaps you've always been emotionally sensitive but never realized the emotions weren't yours—they were mostly the feelings of other people.

Some of us will have physical symptoms, such as being more tired and less focused with lots of brain fog. Of course, those symptoms might also be part of the aging process, or they might be connected to illness, so it's important to always have our physical symptoms evaluated by a professional.

Another interesting sign that you are awakening is a shift in food choices. You might suddenly develop an aversion to sugar or decide to become a vegetarian.

Ultimately, there is no specific way to eat or to *be* during your awakening. Hence, the Akashic Record Keepers always say that our choices are not about being good or bad, right or wrong, but rather about the highest good for your body and soul at this specific time. It's important for you to align to your soul's plan so that you begin to understand the highest and best choices for you as a soul.

Along with physical shifts, such as eating or exercise, awakening people experience heightened emotions. You might find you feel greater compassion and love toward people in your life. In fact, this is one of the beautiful blessings of awakening, and it is helpful to understand that we are transforming as a collective group.

The Akashic Record Keepers say that this process will go on

for many, many years until all of humanity eventually awakens and creates the New Earth. Finding a community of like-minded people can be helpful on your journey. Meditation, yoga, and spending more time in nature also support your awakening. This is your new path—enjoy the journey!

EXERCISE FOR REFLECTION

1. Are you ready to seek the guidance of your soul's plan?

2. Are you ready to lessen your fears and step into your powerful talents and gifts?

3. What questions would you ask the Akashic Masters?

Now, greater awareness of your life purpose and soul plan is available to assist you in creating happiness, health, and fulfillment.

PRAYER TO CLEAR BLOCKS TO AWAKENING

Mother, Father, Goddess, God, please remove and dismantle all structures, barriers, and obstacles holding me back from stepping forward to know Creator/Source.

Please open my heart so I may move into the unified field of Source as I awaken to love and divine grace.

So it is. Blessed Be.

PRAYER TO ACTIVATE THE LOVE WITHIN

Mother, Father, Goddess, God, as I know I am one with you,

I know I am one with the Divine Love vibration, the Golden Energy of Light which is everyone's birthright.

I ask for and receive the Golden Energy of Light as it moves into my crown chakra and slowly moves down into my heart.

I feel this Divine energy move down my arms as it activates my healing channels in my body.

I am a divine servant of Creator and

I am grateful to share this golden light of love.

So it is. Blessed Be.

I am grateful for your interest in learning about your soul plan. In the final chapter, I offer you my concluding thoughts.

CONCLUDING THOUGHTS

Over the years, I have received thousands of messages from the Akashic Record Keepers. They are often answering my questions or helping me to understand life challenges that I've experienced.

Occasionally, they come forward with a request. In 2013, they asked me to author a book for the first time. That time, I replayed, *Ok, what shall we write and how? I have children, and I'm busy with my family.* They gave me two simple steps to follow, and *The Infinite Wisdom of the Akashic Records* came to life. A few years later, they asked me to create a book of healing prayers, which I did.

This time, the Record Keepers said to me:

It's time to help people understand who they truly are. Please help us share the concept of a soul plan and how it informs your life. It is important for people to let go of the idea that we are victims of life. Please help them to understand it is your plan and desire to experience a large variety of situations, challenges and even traumas along with sharing your gifts and your love.

It has been my honor to share the wisdom from the Akashic Records with you at this very important time in history.

Self-Realization

When I was young, I thought self-realization or awakening happened only when one dedicated a lifetime to self-exploration, deep meditation, sacrifice, and servitude. In this life, I chose love and family, which didn't match my idea of the intensity it would take to become enlightened. I was ecstatic when the Akashic Masters told me many years ago, *The Akashic Records are a path to self-realization. One of many ways.*

Since my life has been an incredible journey of trials and tribulations, knowing the Akashic Records could lead me to awakening had me hooked from day one. Thirty years later, I'm still coming back to learn. My journey of awakening has led me to so much more than self.

I loved the idea that maybe I could become enlightened without having to sit and meditate for a lifetime! Plus, every time I've opened my Akashic Records, I have received unconditional love and wisdom, and—when I ask—daily, step-by-step guidance. My journey to self-realization has led me to discover I am truly in my version of heaven on earth.

The Record Keepers remind me on a regular basis that love and forgiveness heal karma and are also a path to awakening. I'm certain many of us have a difficult time forgiving those who have caused us pain, whether physically, emotionally, or psychologically. But we've learned from the Akashic Masters that, to awaken to our pure love and access the full power of unconditional love, we must forgive.

We are standing on a precipice. It might feel scary, confusing, or exciting at times. You have come to experience all that life has to offer and to help humanity awaken.

Your plan was written by your soul to fulfill and complete your soul's desire to grow and share the wisdom it receives from its development.

It is time to release our old ways of being, including our old stories.

Allow yourself to awaken to the love held deeply within your soul. Let that love be the impetus to transform your life.

JOURNAL PAGES

_____

_____

_____

_____

_____

_____

_____

_____

_____

_____

_____

_____

_____

_____

_____

ACKNOWLEDGMENTS

Great gratitude goes out to the Akashic Lords and the Beings of Light who have asked me to bring Akashic Wisdom back to the world. Your pure love, Divine guidance, and profound wisdom have transformed my life.

To Linda Berger, thank you for the edit on all three of my books. You make sense of all the channeled information from the Akashic Masters. You have made this information comprehensible and clear. Your support and love, every day, in so many ways, has opened my heart to a greater depth of receiving. I couldn't have completed this without you.

To my dear husband, Jesse, who has supported me on my spiritual path for over thirty-one years. You make it possible for me to expand into the infinite wisdom of the Akashic Records so that I may teach, write, travel, and share this profound work. Your love assists me in everything I do.

To all my students and clients, whose questions and desires to change their lives have helped me to bring through much of the information you will read in this book.

To my children and all my friends that I haven't mentioned by name, I thank you and I love you. You are the Light that keeps my candle burning. You are the motivation and support that keep me strong. Thank you.

ABOUT THE AUTHOR

Lisa Barnett has devoted her life as a Divine channel of the Akasha, to help people connect to their soul guidance. She is the founder and teacher of Akashic Knowing School of Wisdom, an internationally recognized school where students can learn to access their soul wisdom in their Akashic Records,  along with numerous healing tools, meditation, and prayer systems. Lisa has taught thousands of students worldwide and has helped to train and certify dozens of Akashic consultants and teachers.

She has also spent more than ten years as a Religious Science Certified Practitioner, R.S.C.P., where she offered healing prayer treatment to the congregations of Golden Gate Center for Spiritual Living and served as vice president on the board of directors.

Lisa has more than thirty years of experience in the spiritual healing forum and is a master of many healing modalities. Her specialty is empowering individuals to find greater fulfillment, happiness, abundance, health, and ease by helping them align with their soul path and understand their soul's plan, including soul contracts, karmic patterns, and vows, thereby enabling them to transform with greater ease.

Lisa has developed many amazing programs and books to help people experience lasting transformation, including ten written and auditory courses, dozens of meditations, and frequent webinars to teach people around the world how to access their Akashic Record. The goal of all of these programs and books is to share the tools and prayers from the Akashic Records to help her clients and students, at a soul level, to create the life their hearts and soul's desire.

Find out more at https://akashicknowing.com